NIGERIA: A LAND OF OPPORTUNITIES

Dr Tobi Ilesanmi

DEDICATION

This book is dedicated to my beautiful wife Monisola, my two lovely daughters Jadesola and Busola, the millions of Nigerians, Africans and the entire black world seeking to unearth the huge opportunities around them and move up in the ladder of significance to create sustainable societies that our unborn children will love to call home.

CONTENTS

INTRODUCTION

Nigeria: a land of opportunities? This may likely sound like an irony to a lot of Nigerians. To some nothing good can come out of Nigeria. A lot of people have lost hope in the country. They say since Nigeria is yet to be economically self-sustaining after 53 years of independence, then she can no longer make a head way. We all fold our hands like spectators and pass comments about our oil-rich economy that has been long hobbled by political instability, corruption, and poor management at all levels of leadership characterized by looting and embezzlement of public funds. Political positions are synonymous with wealth. Those who are not opportune to hold political positions feel they have got only one chance at wealth, and that is traveling out of the country.

One of the worst tragedies to happen in Nigeria in recent times is not the looting of federal accounts, but as it were the looting of the human resources going on. One person or the other is traveling out, those still in Nigeria are dreaming of the days they will step their feet on the shores of the United States. The number of relatives abroad has become the standard of gauging the financial well-being of a standard Nigerian family. As one watch Nigerians going in their droves to '*greener pastures*', one cannot but wonder if we are actually getting things right. Instead of going to '*greener pastures*', why not plant your own and keep it green, this will be more dignifying. Slave trade ended more than a century ago, but now we are involved in modern day slavery, people travel out all to end up doing menial jobs abroad. Where is our dignity and self-worth? Immigrants account for a good chunk of poverty abroad. People try to run away from poverty by traveling out of their country but finds themselves wherever they go deeper in poverty, because unknown to them poverty has no geographical boundary!

Our story is just like that of a man in the book *Acres of Diamond¹* who heard that there were diamonds in a far country. He wasn't doing too badly because he had a big parcel of land he was using for farming. Since he really wanted to be extremely wealthy, he decided to go in search of the diamond selling all his property and of course his land. Off he went, he searched and searched until all his money finished. He was soon in rags, and died in poverty.

His successor was going through his garden one day when he noticed a shining piece of black stone, he picked it up and later discovered that it was diamond. They soon found out that there were thousands of such stones in the land. That land became one of the most magnificent diamond mines in history! Often times the things we don't value houses unimaginable treasures, just as the scriptures says,

"But we have this treasure in earthen vessels…"²

There is a treasure inside every man capable of taking him to global prominence. You need not travel abroad to the diamond mines in the far country; all you need is to travel in- broad to release that treasure from within you, and you will soon find out that you are worth much more than all the oil wells in your nation!

Our dignity as blacks is tied to the welfare of our nation and that of the black world at large and not on our individual successes in any part of the world. I am of the opinion that the black man will never gain the respect of the world with accomplishments by blacks under white-controlled systems or sovereignties (including where they claim citizenship). No matter how rich, well-educated, and talented individual black people may be, their collective dignity is tied to the measure of the African continent. The Asians are respected, not because of their individual accomplishments in Europe and America, but rather because of their accomplishment in Asia.

Paul Cuffe (1759-1817), a Quaker businessman, sea captain, patriot and abolitionist of the West African Ashanti descent, was the richest African American in the United States during the early 1800s. Despite the fact that Paul Cuffe was the richest black man and largest black employer in America, he was convinced that no amount of wealth would make a black man socially acceptable in America and that blacks would always be "resident aliens". He felt the only answer was to develop a strong black African nation. Cuffe declared: "Blacks would be better off in Africa, where we can rise to be a people". Hence, he became involved in the British effort to resettle freed slaves to the fledging colony of Sierra Leone, to which he spent a considerable portion of his fortune. I can hear the voice of Cuffe calling on us again to build a strong African nation- Nigeria.

It is true that Nigeria is laden with so many problems, but equally true is that Nigeria is a land of opportunities! In fact Nigeria is another name for opportunities! On every street corner, on every highway you will see opportunities, we even step on them, but we are opportunity blind. This nearness of opportunities in Nigeria has so much paralyzed our senses that we actually mistake them for calamities! We complain about the problems, not recognizing that they are opportunities in disguise! Our greatest opportunity is in our immediate environment. Opportunity is not accessed by an air flight ticket; it is accessed by an open mind.

God did not make a mistake when he created you, tested you positive for performance, and posted you to Nigeria.

"And the Lord God took the man, and put him into the Garden of Eden to dress and to keep it. And the Lord God commanded the man, saying, of every tree of the garden thou mayest freely eat."[3]

The reason why God put his first man in the Garden of Eden was because that was where his assignment and his food were. To think there is another land where you can fully realize your dreams apart from where God placed you is to be deceived! Nigeria is where it is today because we have failed God to keep and dress the garden in which he placed us.

We have lost our sense of dignity and worth as a nation. All we do is blame our government for our predicament, and we refuse to accept responsibility for where we are. Our problem is not due to lack of good leadership, our problem is self-inflicted. Every Nigerian has a role to play, because we have all contributed to our present state one way or the other. Drawing from those words of John F Kennedy during his inaugural address, "Ask not what your country can do for you, ask, what you can do for your country". This should be our mind set in Nigeria if we will ever build a strong economy.

Our problem is not due to lack of good leadership?! Yes, that is true. Someone once said, a people get the kind of leadership they deserve. Or else, we would have placed a demand on our leaders to deliver results. We would have created cultures, values and systems that will make it impossible for a corrupt leader to thrive. But what do we see, we rather demand our own share of the *'national cake'*, hence we built a society and culture that thrives not on excellence and performance but on favoritism and *'connections'*, therefore perpetuating the cycle of mediocrity. Those who are not favored or connected, fold their hands and blame their poverty on the government. I am of the school of thought that believes in the ability of the individual to decide his/her outcome in life the prevailing circumstances notwithstanding. No government can alleviate poverty without addressing the mindset that created it, just like you don't solve a problem with the same mindset that created it. Wealth acquisition is a personal responsibility. You have to take responsibility for the result you get out of life and the one you don't get.

We should always be grieved in our soul when we see our country, and the black world at large represented on the international scene as poor, sickly and inferior breed of humans who need the help of the *'superior'* white nations.

"Then Peter opened his mouth, and said, of a truth I perceived that God is no respecter of persons: But in every nation he that feareth him, and worketh righteousness, is acceptable with him."[4]

Anybody who operates the principles that govern success and wealth acquisition shall be wealthy his geographical location notwithstanding. Anything happening in the US can happen in Nigeria because,

"There is no difference between the Jew and the Greek: for the same Lord over all is rich unto all that call upon him."[5]

There is nothing that makes a white man different from a black man. The only difference between an American and a Nigerian is in the mind. A lot of us believe that some countries and some people are more privileged than us, but that is just a state of mind, in reality we all have equal opportunities irrespective of our location, because,

"...the profit of the earth is for all: the king himself is served by the field."[6]

It doesn't matter where you're located on the earth; your maker said he positioned everybody such that all humans can make profit on this earth. But why is it that some countries and some people are so blessed and others seem barely able to get by. We are beginning to see Nigerians making it to the world's billionaire list. These are people who made their fortune right on the soil of Nigeria, while others are lamenting about the problems, yet the profit of the earth is for all! Every Nigerian has the same God given ability to achieve as much as anybody on earth has achieved without traveling out. Though Nigeria presently has one of the world's highest economic growth rates (averaging 7.4%[7] over the last decade), a well-developed economy with plenty of natural resources, it still retains a high level of poverty, with 63% living on below $1 daily [8], implying a decline and worsening income inequality. Yet, the profit of the earth is for all! I personally feel our inability to see opportunities may be responsible for this.

Nigeria's GDP has grown almost four times from 67.65 billion USD in 2004 to 262.606 billion USD in 2012 within a period of less than 10 years[9].

If Nigeria grows its GDP four times every 10 years, by 2032, Nigeria would reach the same level some G8 member countries are today. This creates a huge opportunity for every Nigerian to improve their wellbeing and create economic boom for themselves. Instead of lamenting that our government has forgotten us, we need to come up with solutions and businesses that will service and meet the needs of the 170 million Nigerians. It's time to move away from a civil service driven economy to a private sector and entrepreneurial driven economy, where even the government will buy needed goods and services predominantly in the private market place.

In the words of President George W Bush on the occasion of the first Trade & Economic Cooperation Forum between the US and Sub-Saharan African countries in October 2001: "No nation in our time has entered the fast track of development without first opening up its economy to world markets." A market based economy is a private sector driven initiative. In this economy, businesses and the individuals they service is king.

 If Nigeria must become a big economy every individual must realize that they have a role to play by ceasing to be dependent on the government and start to bring forth products and services that will solve the numerous problems around. It is high time we realize that wealth acquisition is a personal adventure; it is the responsibility of individuals not the government!
So how can the individuals in Nigeria help move the economy forward?

1

THE PLACE OF VISION

"When I was 19 I caught sight of the future and based my career on what I saw. I turned out to have been right." BILL *GATES*

WHAT IS VISION

Vision is the ability to see. Vision is the picture in the mind of a possible future. It is the knowledge and imagination that are needed in planning for the future with a clear purpose. Vision is the ability to see into the unseen realm. It is an ability to see into the invisible. Vision is the mental conception of a desired future. Vision talks about dreams, imaginations, pictures and sight.

" And the Lord said unto Abram after that Lot was separated from him, lift up now thine eyes, look from the place where thou art northward, and southward, and eastward, and westward: For all the land which thou seest, to thee will I give it, and to thy seed forever."[10]

Vision is the art of lifting up of the eyes and looking to see a well-defined future, the present status notwithstanding. Sight is the ability to see things as they are; vision is the ability to see things as they could be. Sight is a function of the eyes, but vision is a function of the mind. May I ask you a question; have you caught sight of the future? The future Bill Gates saw at the age of 19 is what he is enjoying now. Steve Ballmer, Microsoft CEO, recently said of Microsoft, 'the company had a big vision- to help people realize their full potential, in the earlier days, it was by putting a PC on every desk and in every home'. He said, 'we've come further than we could have imagined, and the impact we have collectively made on the world is undeniable'. He further said, 'I am inspired when talented new hires say they chose Microsoft because they want to change the world'. You can only change your world, your nation and your life with a big vision. What you see today will become your future tomorrow.

LIFE WITHOUT A VISION

The poorest person in the world is not the person without a dime in the bank, but the person without a vision. Vision is the entry permit into the unseen future! Without vision there is no future. As a matter of fact, life is not worth living without a vision. Whatever cannot be conceived cannot be achieved. Where we are as Nigerians today is due to our lack of vision. We've not seen a better future that's why we've remained on the same spot. God told Abraham, what you see is what you get, that is, you see nothing you get nothing, you see poverty you get poverty. That is the Law of Visions and Dreams. Nobody, no institution, and no Nation will ever arrive at a future they have not seen. No woman ever delivers a baby without conception. Vision is the womb that births the future. Whatever cannot be conceived cannot be achieved.

"Where there is no vision, the people perish: but he that keepeth the law, happy is he."[11]

All the things that produce a happy Nations, such as wealth, state of the art infrastructures, security of lives and property and good governance all hinges on this Law. The fact that the population of Nigerians below the poverty line is about 63% proves that we're not keeping the Law. Can you imagine trying to navigate in the ocean without a compass, or trying to drive a car at night without a headlamp? That's an accident going to happen! That is how it is trying to live life without a vision. Living without a vision is like playing a football match without a goal post, I mean it is a complete waste of time, and energy.

THE INVISIBLE COMES BEFORE THE VISIBLE

Lack of vision will always produce a life full of lacks, because, the visible is controlled from the invisible realm. When there is nothing in the invisible (vision), there will be nothing in the real world. An empty mind will produce an empty life. That you are broke and have no money today might be because you were mentally broke yesterday!

The invisible, the intangible has far greater value than the visible. The greatest asset of a lot of the fortune 500 companies is not in the tangibles like plants, buildings, but in the intangibles- brand, trademark and overall business concept. For instance the Coca-Cola, a name that is more commonly recognized than any other in the world, has a brand value that is almost equal to the overall asset value of the Coca-Cola Company. Similarly, Apple, a company that has captured the imagination of the world, inspired such devotion and revolutionized the way we live, is not really defined by products, but by a certain way of thinking, a certain set of values, and an unmistakable human touch that pervades everything Apple does.

As revealed in a study by an IP attorney, intangible assets became a powerful force in the latter third of the 20th century. He discovered that at the end of the 1970s, corporate balance sheet was represented by 80% tangible assets and 20% intangible. But in 30 years, by 1997, the ratio of assets had essentially inverted to 73% intangible and the rest tangible. Great enterprises, great societies are built on visions that transcend the tangible, but end up impacting on the tangibles.

"Through faith we understand that the worlds were framed by the word of God, so that the things which are seen were not made of things which do appear."[2]

Everything came from the invisible. The tangibles came into existence by the operation of the intangibles, so the latter has far greater value than the former. There was a time when there was nothing. God was all by himself; the only thing God had then was an idea. All the big global corporations, the world's tallest buildings started with an idea in the mind. To have an empty mind without the faintest idea of the future is worse than having an empty bank account! It is always a great challenge to see beyond your present circumstances, but that is what distinguishes you as a front liner in the race of life.

"The Lord possessed me in the beginning of his way, before his works of old. I was set up from the everlasting, from the beginning, or ever the earth was. When there were no depths, I was brought forth..."[3]

God created the world and all its treasures from nothing as it were. There was a time when Bill Gates had no money I mean none, he had no inheritance, his parents were not the super-rich, but he had a vision and *saw* himself dominating the world. He was quoted sometimes ago when referring to a recent meeting with Paul Allen his friend together with whom he founded Microsoft, "We like to talk about how the fantasies we had as kids actually came true."[14] Wealth creation starts from the mind. We'll never arrive at a future we've not seen. Without a clear mental picture of a desired future no one ever rises.

THE SINGAPORE STORY

Tiny City state Singapore with a population of about 5.31 million (3 times smaller than Lagos State) has no natural resources. No wonder few gave them a chance of survival when it was granted independence in 1965, 5 years after Nigeria got her own. But their founding father Lee Kuan Yew chose to believe in the intangibles. He knew that every great achievement starts as a dream before becoming a reality. He had a vision for a state that would not simply survive but prevail by excelling. Superior intelligence, discipline and ingenuity (intangibles) would substitute for resources.

Immediately, they set up the Economic Development Board, charged with formulating economic strategies, focusing on promoting Singapore's manufacturing sector. The results were the industrial estates that helped attracted foreign investment. The progress as at mid-1970 made Singapore the third largest oil-refining center in the world, even though they didn't have any natural resources. The Housing Development Board developed huge building projects, which with the Central Provident Fund Housing Scheme helped resettled almost the entire population in affordable, modern apartments. The Singapore of today stands as a testament. They have the world's number one airline, best airport, and busiest port of trade. It is the high tech leader of Southeast Asia and has the one of the world's highest per capital real income, having grown from less than $1,000 at independence to over $50,000 in 2012.

THE AMERICAN DREAM

The US was once referred as the Wild- Wild West. But their forefathers decided to take responsibility for the future giving birth to the American dream. [15] What is the American dream? It is what every American aspires to achieve. The dream was defined as, "Political and religious freedom, equal access to education, equal opportunity in the workplace and ultimately success and wealth." Today, America is seen as an epitome of wealth, success opportunity and globally accepted as the world's policeman. The American economy wields more power than the whole of the European Union!

If America and Singapore stated with a dream, may I ask, what is the Nigerian dream? When are we going to create the Nigerian dream? When are we going to stop dreaming of the day we will leave our country to "greener pastures"? It's time to stop dreaming of traveling out. It's time to dream of creating "green pastures" in our own country. How can we be so shallow minded to think we can't create our own success story that will match and even surpass that of America or Singapore. It is time to create the Nigerian Dream.

VISION AND THE NEXT GENERATION

What Abraham saw became the inheritance of thousands of generations after him. Vision has the ability to transform a man into a generational phenomenon. The impact of such a life last for a thousand generations.

"He hath remembered his covenant forever, the word which he commanded to a thousand generations. Which covenant he made with Abraham and his oath unto Isaac...?"[6]

A dream always outlives the dreamer. For your name to end and not be remembered for anything when you leave this earth is a proof that you have lived a visionless life! Although the visionaries that shape world history have died long ago they still wield more power than many people walking on the earth, because the world is run on their ideas. In all higher institutions of learning we learn about ideas propounded by people who are dead. We even dream of working for their companies and we idealize their products.

I believe just as God told Abraham, God is also telling us to lift up now our eyes from the place where we are and see a future that does not yet exist, whatever we see now will be the lot of the remaining generation of Nigerians and the black world at large. I believe we are the generation saddled with the responsibility of deciding the destiny of the future generation of Africans.

"But many that are first shall be last; and the last shall be first."[7]

Baton must always be passed from one hand to the other. Empires have always come and gone. There is nothing that says that a third world nation cannot become a first world nation. As a matter of fact the above scripture talks of the possibility of such phenomenal turnaround! And it doesn't have to take a whole generation to achieve that. Tiny Singapore with no natural resources moved from being a third world nation to a first world nation within a period of 30 years. So, Nigeria can do the same even within a shorter time. But, we must conceive it and believe it first before we'll ever handle it.

"And the sons of Ham; Cush, and Mizraim, and Phut, and Canaan...And Cush begat Nimrod: he began to be mighty one in the earth. He was a mighty hunter before the Lord: wherefore it was said, Even as Nimrod the mighty hunter before the Lord. And the beginning of his kingdom was Babel, and Erech, and Accad, and Calneh, in the land of Shinar. Out of that land went forth Ashur, and builded Nineveh, and the city Rehoboth, and Calah, and Resen between Nineveh and Calah: the same is a great

city."[18]
"And the Lord came down to see the city and the tower which the children of men builded."[19]

Blacks and the people who settled in Africa after the flood were descendants of Ham, one of Noah's sons.[20]The most magnificent edifice and city to be attempted by man, that moved the Almighty God to come and have a look was the brainwork of the Hamitic people. The famous Christian anthropologist Arthur C. Constance, states that all the earliest civilization of note were founded and carried to the highest technical proficiency by Hamitic people.[20]Scientists have proved it through archeological studies that the most ancient civilization on the earth was in Africa. Africa was a Mecca for scholars from other parts of the world, where many Greek scholars, to whom the world now credits the origin of many frontiers of knowledge, studied. We now know that the oldest Mathematics texts (over 4000 years old)-The Rhind, Berlin, and Moscow papyri were all excavated from Africa. The greatest Mathematician Euclid was born in Africa 2330 years ago; he studied in Africa, taught in Africa, lived in Africa, and died in Africa without traveling even once out of Africa![21] Can't you see that right at the root of the black race is greatness? So, why do we have this inferiority mentality? It is time to get rid of such a mentality, and aim for greatness.

The first man God created called Adam may have been black, because the word Adam came from the Hebrew word that means 'red earth'. In fine art brown and black are two colors that mean earth. Native Americans thought black was good because it was the color of the soil, which gives life. Black is not a color, strictly speaking. It is the absence of all colors. Black absorbs all aspects and shades of light. It conceals and contains all colors. So if God wants to create a single man that will bring forth all the other men of different colors, it's just logical that he'll make him black, because black contain all colors. So black is the original. There is no reason why a black man should feel inferior just because of his skin color. As a matter of fact we should have a superiority mentality because there is no way a copy image can match up with the original! It's now the turn of the black world to enjoy phenomenal economic transformation. Now I want you to take a trip into the future, what can you see? Remember,

"All the land which thou seest to thee will I give it and to your seed forever" [10]

It is time to see our economy emerging as one of the greatest world economies. I can hear somebody saying, greatest world economies? Do you think all the others will be sleeping? What happens to the others is not our business. God did not tell Abraham to watch out for the philistine, he simply said look from where you are and all you see is all you will have. I believe after a person has failed so much just as we have in Nigeria, that person should come up with a vow and determination to achieve outstanding success so that he can revenge on failure. Don't you think we have to revenge on poverty in the black world? Are you not tired of the international identity of poverty that we have?

I don't know what you see, but I can see Nigeria becoming one of the largest world economies! I can see the next generation of billionaires rise from Nigeria! I'm not talking about those who stole and stack up money in foreign banks. You are a spoilt brat if you think you cannot make a lot of money in Nigeria without resorting to stealing. As a matter of fact I believe you can make enough money in Nigeria that the Nigerian government will have to sign a MOU with your company because of your relevance! You don't have to be in government, or rely only on government contracts. Note that a number of people are already demonstrating this right on the soil of Nigeria, creating multinational giants that are meeting the needs of people all over Africa and the rest of the world. At the same Nation, where you were lamenting and criticizing the government, they simply sat down to solve a portion of the problem and today we have such men been listed on the Forbes list of the World's Wealthiest men.

IMAGINATION

Imagination is the art of forming images of the invisible in the mind. Imagination is the creative force of God at work in mortal men. Whatever you imagine, whether good or bad eventually happens. Imagination is the art of creating what does not yet exist through mental projections.

"And they said, one to another, Go to, let us build us a city and a tower, whose top may reach up to heaven; and let us make us a name, lest we be scattered abroad upon the face of the earth. And the Lord said, Behold, the people are one, and they have all one language; and this they begin to do: and now nothing will be restrained from them, which they have imagined to do."[22]

Note that at this time civilization was in its earliest stage, yet God said if they imagine building such a massive edifice he himself would not be able to stop them! God did not allow them because his plan was for humans to spread throughout the surface of the earth. Now that God's plan is for the last to be the first, we too can say, go to, let us build us a Nigeria whose economy will be the largest in the world, so that we'll revenge on our past failures and poverty and bring glory back to this continent. Instead of wishing we were born in the US, I believe it's time to use our imagination to create a new Nigeria that will match and surpass the US in all things.

The power of imagination is illustrated even in Animals!

"And Jacob took him rods of green poplar, and of the hazel and chestnut tree; and pilled white strakes in them, and made the white appear which was in the rods. And he set the rods, which he had pilled before the flocks in the gutters in the watering troughs when the flocks came to drink, that they should conceive when they come to drink. And the flocks conceived before the rods, and brought forth cattle ringstraked, speckled, and spotted. And Jacob did separate the lambs, and set the faces of the flock towards the ringstraked, and all the brown in the flock of Laban; and he put his own flocks by themselves, and put them not unto Laban's cattle. And it came to pass, whensoever the stronger cattle did conceive, that Jacob laid the rods before the eyes of the cattle in the gutters that they might conceive among the rods."23

As the animals mate before the spotted rods, they saw the spotted rods, created a mental picture of a ringstraked, speckled, and spotted offspring, and eventually brought forth such animals as they have imagined! You will always become what you imagine yourself to be whether good or bad! It is a universal law that what you see is what you get. What we imagine eventually becomes a reality, because,

"As he thinketh in his heart so is he..."24

What are your thoughts about Nigeria? As Nigerians think in their heart so they are. Someone said, "If you think you can't you're right, if you think you can, you're also right." The problem is not with our weather, we have all year round summer the only problem we have is in the mind. Our thoughts has held us in captivity to the point that we have helped to perpetuate the brain drain subtly, tagged American Visa lottery.

SEEING OPPORTUINITIES IN NIGERIA

It has been said that eyes that look are many but eyes that see are few. A lot of us look at Nigeria as a land of numerous problems in fact we have all become economic problems analysts. But we fail to realize that behind every problem is an opportunity. Here is a story culled from the book "The Principles and Power of Vision."25

"There is the story of a man and his friend who visited India years ago.

They were walking down the streets of Bombay and saw the thousands of poor people on the streets. Hundreds lay on cardboard boxes in the gutters or under the bridges. Filthy people were begging along the streets. There were poor people by thousands walking barefoot.

The man said to his friend, "Look at these people. Isn't it a sad sight? They're without shoes. Thousands of barefoot people. What a pity. Isn't it a shame that we have so much at home in our country while these people are poor and without shoes. I will never forget this sight. I have to tell my wife about this." He continued to talk about how poor they were and about their bare feet. By this time his friend had already taken out a piece of paper and was writing down some notes. He had started working out a plan of how to ship shoes over to India and how to manufacture shoes in India. Instead of saying, "Look at the bare feet," he was saying, "Look at the feet that need shoes!" Today his enterprise is one of the largest shoe companies in America. One man saw bare feet. Another saw an opportunity for a much needed business." It's all in how you see."

"Moreover the word of the Lord came unto me, saying, Jeremiah, what seest thou? And I said, I see a rod of an almond tree. Then said the Lord unto me, Thou hast well seen for I will hasten my word to perform it.'[26]

Whatever mental picture we have of our nation is the future we will have because God is only committed to what we see. I see Nigeria and the whole of Africa as a virgin land, where there are all manner of untapped opportunities! You don't need to do expensive market surveys to recognize the needs in Africa, all you need to do is identify any of our numerous problems and begin to solve them and you would have created a money-spinning machine for your generation! Even a blind man can make money in Nigeria! Can you imagine what we do, we leave all our problems here unsolved and we go begging at the corridor of the white nations.

If all those people traveling out just solved a problem for the 170 million Nigerians, and charge $10 per month, that will be about $1.7 billion in revenue per month, by the time investors" money, and the cost of solving that problem is deducted the minimum the company will be netting is a whopping $100 million per month and close to a $1 billion per annum! Can you now see that right on the soil of Nigeria, you can replicate what any fortune 500 company is doing. What I'm saying is that the opportunities in Nigeria are so huge that it will be insanity to leave them and saddle your horse in search of diamonds in the far country!

The sad part is that the whole world is upbeat about the huge investment opportunities in Nigeria and the rest of Africa, while Africans themselves are still oblivious of the opportunities. I read an article recently, titled 'Why Nigerians Diaspora won't return home'. The author claims political instability, lack of infrastructure, lack of security of lives and property and the comfort of being overseas as compared to Nigeria are some of the reasons. But, I feel those are the same reasons why we should have a brain gain from those in diaspora, since they may be better positioned to solve these problems and replicate the same quality of societal life they have seen worked abroad while also creating fortune for themselves. But, they are opportunity blind, similar to the man in the story '*Acres of Diamond*'.

What can you see? Can you now see opportunities in Nigeria? The whole world has suddenly woken up to the huge opportunities the next frontier-Africa presents, and every business that wants to have double digit growth must become a player in Africa. There is already a gold rush with the mantra '*Africa Rising*' among the global investment community, since more than half of the world's fastest growing economies are in Africa. If we don't take the bull by the horn and spearhead this investment band wagon, we may not benefit maximally from this opportunity, because of the risk of subtle re-colonization and exploitation.

A business report in 2005, chronicled how Equatorial Guinea, a rich country was stripped of its wealth. BG Plc, formerly British Gas, was buying up nearly 60m tones of liquefied natural gas- the entire planned output for 17 years of Equatorial Guinea's new LNG plant, an amount that was worth $15 billion. The government of Equatorial Guinea may see little more than $65 million a year from the LNG deal, whilst it was allowed only 25% share in the LNG plant itself. What allowed such a deal was some dirty shades of bribe and corruption all through the chain of the deal. It is indeed dangerous to be oblivious of the numerous opportunities in your immediate environment, because before you wake up, smarter and aggressive businesses from other parts of the world will take them up leaving you with the crumbs to pick! Individual Nigerians have a greater role to play in developing the economy than even the federal government. That's why there is a responsibility on you to see opportunities in Nigeria.

Just as Abraham was given the responsibility of deciding the destiny of his future generation by seeing into the future, I believe we have a responsibility of creating a dream for New Nigeria, a Land of opportunities. The question now is what can we see ourselves achieving in the next 5 years, 10 years, and 20 years and so on? Where we are is what we saw years back and our future hinges on what vision is in our hearts today. Now is the time to start dreaming a better future than our present states. It is time to stop blaming our government and our leaders we must accept responsibility everybody should have a dream of a great future for the nation. It's time we begin to see ourselves making a major contribution to national development. This syndrome of blaming the government for our financial predicament must stop.

There are several corporations in the US that earn more revenue than many nations in Africa. All these corporations are owned by people, so we too should see ourselves owning multinational giants. Whatever is too big for your mind to capture will be too big for your hand to handle. Remember that there is no difference between Bill Gates, Michael Dell, Warren Buffet and any Nigerian residence in Nigeria, because God made all of us in his image and *the profit of the earth is for all!* Start seeing yourself achieving extraordinary success against all odds.

We must stop looking unto the government; we're the one that the government should look up to. We're not less human than the guys above, we also have corporations packaged and buried in us. We must release our full worth. Africa is long overdue for a change! That you have nothing, and you're all by yourself is no news, even God in the beginning was all by himself, he had nothing except a dream of what he wanted to create. Your full worth is not measured in terms of what is around you now; your worth is actually measured in terms of the size of your heart. Your life will never grow bigger than the dreams in your heart. So what have you seen?

DREAMS

A life of outstanding success, a nation of glory, all begins from a dream in the heart. We all can invent our own future by conceiving a clearly specific and highly ambitious dream.

"And Joseph dreamed a dream, and he told it his brethren: and they hated him yet the more. And he said unto them, hear I pray you, this dream that I have dreamed….. And he dreamed yet another dream, and told it his brethren, and said, Behold, I have dreamed a dream" [27]

This dreamy visionary was so convinced of his idea of the future that he couldn't help but tell his folks who hated him. A dream has the ability of intoxicating the dreamer conditioning his words and actions!

"And they said one to another, Behold, this dreamer cometh. Come now therefore let us slay him, and cast him into some pit, and we will say, some evil beast hath devoured him: and we shall see what shall become of his dreams."[28]

Despite the attempt of his folks to abort his dream, all they could do is move him closer to his dreamland. Nobody, no adverse circumstances can stop a dreamer! Remember even God said,

"… and now nothing will be restrained from them which they have imagined to do."[22]

When you become a dreamer you become invincible.

"And Joseph was the governor over the land, and he it was that sold to all the people of the land: and Joseph's brethren came and bowed down themselves before him with their faces to the earth…And Joseph remembered the dreams which he dreamed of them…"[29]

There is nothing so awesome and fulfilling than to see ourselves living in the reality of yesterday's dreams, fantasies and mental pictures. Indeed dreams do come true! Someone once said, "One of the most accurate ways of predicting the future is to invent it." You invent the future by dreaming.

VISION AND LEADERSHIP

Vision is the source of true leadership. Everybody is a leader in his vision, because he is the one who can make the future he has conceived to happen. Vision is given to individuals, not communities. All through scriptures we see God sparking up a dream in the heart of different individuals, who ended up being the leader for that particular mission. Although no man can fulfill a vision single handedly, a vision is given to an individual first who in turn transfer the vision to others.

"I will stand upon my watch, and set me upon the tower, and will watch to see what he will say unto me, and what I shall answer when I am reproved. And the Lord answered me, and said, write the vision, and make it plain upon tables, that he may run that readeth it."[30]

"I will", not "we will". Every Nigerian has the responsibility of watching to see what the future holds for them. Remember the word, eyes that looks are many but eyes that see are few. Those who see usually end up as generational phenomenal leaders, just like Bill Gate who is now regarded as the master of the Information Age. From the above scripture, a visionary is responsible for documenting his vision, which is the only means of passing the vision to others who will help with its fulfillment. Documenting the vision helps to create a mission statement that can serve as the constitution for that individual, that business, that community and that nation.

What is the role of leadership in birthing a Nigerian dream? What Nigeria need are visionaries. We don't need politicians; we only need people who can create a dream and then transfer that dream into the mind of the people. A leader is someone who can conceive an idea of the desired future that does not exist and transfer the same into others with a burning passion for the fulfillment of the same. A leader is not someone who can use money to bribe his way to positions of power, as we do in Nigeria. A leader is someone who can set evolutionary or revolutionary goal and yet convince others that such hairy audacious goal is a possibility, since mega-prizes are only possible with mega-aims! A leader is someone who has a well-defined conception of the desired future, and has the ability to influence others with the same carrying them along on a journey of fulfillment.

"And Caleb stilled the people before Moses, and said, Let us go up at once, and possess it; for we are well able to overcome it."[31]

Leaders believe so much in what they see that they are ready to stick out their neck for it and convince the people that a seemingly impossible task is possible. For someone to claim he's a leader and does not even have a clear-cut insight into the future that doesn't exist, such a one is fooling himself. It is the responsibility of the leaders to impart vision into the minds the followers.

2

THE PLACE OF PASSION

"Our lives begin to end when we become silent about things that matter." _Martin Luther king Jr.

WHAT IS PASSION?

Passion is a very strong deeply felt emotion of love, anger, or belief in an idea or principle. Passion is also a strong liking for something. Passion is the combination of love and hate. We hate what gives us pain, and we love whatever gives us pleasure. Man is designed to be motivated by two emotions: pleasure and pain. We move towards anything that gives us deep pleasure and run away from anything that gives us pain. Pain is a sensation of deep displeasure or an emotion that hurts. Pain is also a deep sensation of discomfort. Pain is an emotional experience that signals potential damage to the body so the body tends to run away from such stimuli.

What a man is running towards is an indication of what he's running away from. He hates where he's coming from so much so that he's ready to give it all it takes to get to the other side. Or, he loves where he's heading for so much so that he's willing to pay the price. Have you seen something you love so much in your mind that you're willing to pay the price for? There is a story of Jacob and Rachel in the bible, Jacob loved Rachel so much so that he was willing to work without salary for 14 years, so that he could marry her! What do you love to see happen in Nigeria? Or, what is it in Nigeria that is causing you heartaches and pain? God created those emotions to motivate us to take the actions required to bring us fulfillments. Every major achievement hinges on this principle of love and hate.

A HEART FOR A CAUSE OTHER THAN SELF

"And they said unto me, the remnants that are left of the captivity there in the province are in great affliction and reproach: the wall of Jerusalem also is broken down, and the gates thereof are burned with fire. And it came to pass when I heard these words, that I sat down and wept, and mourned certain days, and fasted and prayed before the God of

heaven… And it came to pass in the month Nisan, in the twentieth year of Artaxerxes the king that wine was before him: and I took up the wine, and gave it unto the king. Now I had not been beforetime sad in his presence. Wherefore the king said unto me, why is thy countenance sad, seeing thou art not sick? This is nothing else but sorrow of heart. Then I was sore afraid… Then I said unto the king, If it pleased the king, and if thy servant has found favor in thy sight that thou wouldest send me unto Judah unto the city of my father's sepulchers, that I may build it."[32]

You've heard all manner of news about the state of utter decadence in your country, yet you're not moved. You have watched in the media and have seen our international identity of poverty, yet it doesn't bug you. You've seen mass unemployment; you've seen all manner of problems in the country yet your heart is not pricked. You claim, I work for so and so firm, I earn good money in so and so country, I'm not really affected, so far I can take care of my family, I think I'm ok. Nehemiah was working for the White House of his days, obviously he was well paid, yet a report of the problems in his home country made him to weep and mourn certain days! May I ask you a question where is your heart? Nehemiah was ready to risk his life by being sad before the king because of the evil news he heard from home. What are you living for? You sure won't go far if you're living for yourself!

"And as he talked with them, behold, there came up the champion, the Philistine of Gath, Goliath by name out of the armies of the Philistines and spake according to the same words: and David heard them. And all men of Israel when they saw the man, fled from him, and were sore afraid. And the men of Israel said, have you seen this man that is come up? Surely to defy Israel is he come up: and it shall come to pass that the man who killeth him, the king will enrich him with great riches, and will give him his daughter, and make his father's house free in Israel. And David spake to the men that stood by him, saying, what shall be done to the man that killeth this Philistine, and taketh away the reproach from Israel? For who is this uncircumcised Philistine, that he should defy the armies of the living God?"[33]

David wasn't even in the Army, he was just passing by, and he heard Goliath humiliating the armies of the living God, immediately his passion was fueled. He just couldn't stand watching the humiliation and reproach of his country, he had to do something. At the age 17, when all the men of war were sore afraid, this boy just couldn't contain it anymore he had to move into the scene, putting his life on the line! You've heard of how situations and circumstances are humiliating your country yet it hasn't crossed your mind that you could make a contribution to solving any of the problems.

You claim you're not in government, or you claim you're still young.

There is a specific problem in Nigeria God has ordained you to solve. I mean there is a Goliath that has been harassing your nation ever since. You have all it takes to solve the problem, why do you want to deny your nation of that solution. When you solve that problem your life assumes a new status all together, and you enjoy such wealth you never thought possible. You are not after the reward; you are just passionately driven to enhance the well-being of others.

Without true love in your heart for your nation you will not see the opportunities there. Love aims at providing solutions to problems. It takes a heart to make a mark on the earth. It's your passion for your nation that gives you your place in that nation. Passion for others propels you for a life of outstanding accomplishment. It's your passion that determines your portion in any nation. Passion makes you think in terms of what contribution you're going to make. Passion is a driving force for great achievement.

Passion unlocks keenness of imagination, courage, will power, persistence and creative abilities which are the attributes required to attain greatness in all areas of human endeavor. Passion is the fuel for irresistible pursuit. Passion propels an individual, an organization, and a nation from the present to the future they have seen. The reason why Nigeria and Africa at large has remained on this shameful spot is because both the leaders and the followers have no heart for their nation and the continent.

Can you explain why a leader should loot the nations treasury and store the money in foreign banks. That's the same thing an animal will do! How do you also explain the level of excitement people express when they're planning to travel out of the country permanently? Everybody is complacent; we're all in survival mood, failing to realize that when you live for a cause other than yourself your life will assume a new order of fulfillment. To be in survival mood is to be struggling to exist and not die despite difficulties. That is the lowest form of life and it is used in reference to animals, in which when an animal has its own bread and water, everything is okay for that animal, the others can go and die! We're not animals in Africa, why are we behaving like one? When you begin to live for others certain issues of your life such as food, shelter, clothing and everything that makes for good life, no longer become a concern to you because they are made cheaply available to you.

"And the Lord planted a garden eastward in Eden: and there he put the man whom he

had formed....And the Lord took the man, and put him into the garden of Eden to dress it and to keep it. And the Lord commanded the man saying, of every tree of the garden thou mayest freely eat."[3]

Man was not created to look for food and the good things of life as we do today, we were created to just keep and dress the garden in which God placed us and our food comes spontaneously from the garden we're keeping. That means if we can have a sense of stewardship to keep and to dress this garden-Nigeria and Africa, our food will naturally come on its own (freely) from the land without sweat! Note that man is not the owner of the garden he was commanded to keep, so living for a cause other than self is the key to wealth!

MEETING THE NEEDS OF THE MAJORITY

"For after all these things do the gentiles seek: For your heavenly father knoweth that ye have need of these things. But seek ye first the kingdom of God and his righteousness; and all these things shall be added unto you."[34]

So, the shortest cut to wealth if there is any is not to deprive others of their share of things, but putting their welfare before yours! Let me show you how this will work, even in business. If your primary aim of going into that business is to genuinely meet the needs of the masses, and you deliver far more than you promised, you won't need any prayer for the money to start flowing to you, but if you go primarily to meet your own personal needs you won't last long on the stage, because market forces will soon push you off. Show me any business that puts customers first, where the customers are always right, it's just a matter of time that business will soon own the largest market share.

Henry Ford saw a need; at that time automobiles were only made for the super-rich, so, his thoughts were more cars for more people. He therefore decided to build cars that millions of people could afford- a family car at an honest price. As a result he invented the process of mass assembly of automobiles; build a company that is still vibrant today after 100 years, and of course became the richest man in the world! All the car companies of that time that refused to change to meeting the needs of the masses were either bought over or went out of business. Selfishness is a plague worse than HIV infection! Your life cannot rise more than the level of your commitment to others. Every self-oriented dream will soon kill the dreamer. There was the story of the rich fool in the Bible, he was all out to possess everything for himself, it was at a point when he wanted to possess his soul that God, "said it is enough, you can possess all the other things but the soul is mine, so let me have it!"

Nigeria is presently sitting on a growing housing deficit of 17 million housing units, with more than 70% of Nigerians presently living in sub-standard or sub-human accommodation. The United Nations estimated that Nigeria's population would reach 289 million by 2050, during which Nigeria's housing deficit will be around 30 million housing units. The success and sustainability of a society is not measured on the wellbeing of the 5% upper class, it is measured on how it takes care of the masses, the underprivileged and the majority at the bottom of the pyramid. Entrepreneurs and developers with a heart for a cause other than self can meet this need profitably, by creating new cities, new sustainable societies and contribute to building a nation our unborn children will love to call home.

Everybody celebrates Bill Gates as the richest man on earth today, but his drive wasn't to be the richest as it were, one of his drives was a passion to see a computer in every home and on every desk on the earth! [35] Bill Gate, regarded as the world's most generous person, says that as long as he helps eradicate deadly diseases like polio and malaria, he doesn't care if he is forgotten after his death! Gates has already given more than $28 billion within just 5 years of starting Bill and Melinda Gates Foundation, but said the total amount invested is less important than precise measures of impact, like child mortality! [36] That is a man with a heart for others. But you, your dream is to travel out, and be just comfortable the others can die if they like! That's the animal way, sure not the way for those who will control the wealth of the world. Our thoughts as Nigerians should be more than just for survival; we should incorporate others in our dream. It's time for us as Nigerians to think in terms of what we want to give rather what we want to get.

Bishop Oyedepo, said, *"A millionaire is not someone who has accumulated a million dollar, a millionaire is someone who has affected a million others!"* It's impossible to successfully affect a million people positively and still be poor, the least you'll be is a million dollar man. In the global business world, the success of most corporations is measured in terms of their market share, which is the percentage of a given population that has been influenced and has become loyal customers of that business.

"There is he that scattereth, and yet increaseth; and there is that withholdeth more than it meet, but it tendeth to poverty. The liberal soul shall be made fat: and he that watereth

shall be watered also himself." [37]

Those who want to be blessed live their lives as a reservoir of blessing to others. The size of your heart towards others determines the size of your business coast. God increases your blessing in the proportion to which you're ready to be a blessing to others. God told Abraham,

"... I will bless thee, and make thy name great; and thou shall be a blessing:" [38]

The owner of Silver and Gold guides his thing only to where it will be accessible to more and more people; he only guides his wealth to people who are *reservoirs*. The money spent in a country is described as its currency (from Middle English *curraunt*, meaning circulation), because it circulates from one person to the other, as a medium of exchange for goods and services. Goods and services are far more important than the money. So, anyone who really wants the money, must not focus on the money, but focus on the people who needs goods and services, who will in turn bring the money. There is a way a person in business will relate with the people such that there won't be the need to beg them to drop their money; the reverse will be the case. When you offer people what they really need, they will hand over that *'worthless'* banknote to you, to take up from you the more *valuable* services and goods.

The whole investment community belief there is a rising income level in Nigeria, suggesting a maturation of the middle class. Total consumer spending in Nigeria in 2010 was estimated to be $115 billion and is expected to rise significantly in the coming years. Little wonder many multinational retailers are making entry into more Nigerian cities, hoping to tap into this opportunity, while also changing the shopping landscape and giving indigenous retail outlets stiff competition. One of the leading retailers in Africa- Shoprite, a brand of choice for many consumers across the African continent fully understands the needs and wants of shoppers. They have positioned themselves to service more and more people with their large shopping space, offer the widest range of products, and the highest standard of freshness and quality whilst maintaining the lowest prices. The moment you sincerely build a business to service more and more people without excluding those at the bottom of the pyramid, your chance of wealth creation will grow in geometric proportion!

ADDING VALUE TO OTHERS

"And there was a strife among them, which of them should be accounted the greatest. And he said unto them, the king of the gentiles exercise lordship over them; and they that exercise authority over them are called benefactors. But ye shall not be so: but he that is greatest among you let him be as the younger; and he that is chief, as he that doth serve. For weather is greater, he that sitteth at meat, or he that serveth? Is not he that sitteth at meat? But I am among you as he that serveth."[39]

Jesus is saying when you are all out to serve others with your business or career instead of exploiting them, you will emerge the greatest in your world! In the business world, revenue and profit is determined by value added to the customer after using the product and services. The more value a product or a service adds to the customer, the more the patronage, and the more the returns on investment. To have a customer focused corporate culture is to be a market leader, and to have a money focused corporate culture is to be a market looser.

You can't be truly in love with others and not live glorious. You can't live a frustrated life loving genuinely. You don't die living in love, even if it means giving everything plus your own life. Remember Jesus, he loved and loved until he had to give his life, and so since 3000 years ago, the world is yet to recover from the impact of his life! Sure Jesus is the greatest businessman who ever lived! Imagine starting a business just with 12 employees and now having over 2 billion employees! That business has spanned more than 30 centuries yet it remains the market leader! Your actual lifespan is not determined by your physical heartbeat, but your heart beat towards others. There are people though dead long ago, they still wield more control in world affairs than those physically living, because of the contributions they made when they were alive. Passion is what makes you spot a need and commit yourself to meeting it.

PASSION FOR A CAUSE

Men of greatest achievement are men of deep passion for a particular cause. Men who have accumulated great fortunes and achieved outstanding recognition in any area of human endeavors are men who were deeply passionately involved with what they were doing. The founding fathers of the US poured their hearts into their country creating the American dream, which gave birth to America, as we know it today. Every generation is meant to be an improvement on the previous. We're the generation conferred with the responsibility of deciding the lot of our unborn children. We cannot afford to fold our hands as if it doesn't concern us.

The scripture says, "Woe to them that are at ease in Zion and trust in the mountain of

Samaria…" [40]

When you're complacent despite obvious needs, problems, and Goliaths, the scripture says you attract a curse! Remember that word from Martin Luther King Jr., "Our lives begin to end when we become silent about the things that matter!" The things happening in our land should fuel our passion for seeing changes by stimulating our creativity. It is time for all of us whether small or great, rich or poor, old or young to begin to think in terms of what we want to give to our nation. It's time we stop thinking about what our nation is going to give to us. Let's stop thinking of sharing the *'national cake'*. Imagine sharing the same cake for 53 years! It may finish sooner than we thought! Let's start thinking on baking our own individual cakes big enough to share with other nations.

"And the Jews Passover was at hand, and Jesus went up to Jerusalem, And found in the Temple those that sold oxen and sheep and doves, and changers of money sitting: And when he made a scourge of small cords, he drove them out of the temple, and the sheep, and the oxen; and poured out the changers' money, and overthrew the tables; And said unto them that sold doves, Take these things hence; make not my Father's house an house of merchandise. And his disciples remembered that it was written, the zeal of thine house hath eaten me up" [41]

I can imagine Jesus with a consuming passion, beating and driving out those guys, from the temple, indeed, men of passion are men of outstanding accomplishment. Jesus did not stay afar off to criticize them, and David did not stay miles away criticizing the expertise of Saul's Army, they both went into action to restore the lost dignity and honor. We need not complain or criticize the government and everybody, all we need is to get up on our feet and begin to contribute. If you don't want poverty to eat you up, it's time to be eaten up for a cause other than self-restoring the lost dignity of Nigeria and the black world at large!

3

PRODUCTS AND SERVICES

"Unless your vision translates into a marketable product or service, it has no value."
Robert Heller.

WHAT ARE PRODUCTS AND SERVICES?

Products and services are tangible and intangible commodities brought forth into existence by both mental and physical activities, with the aim of meeting a need and generating profit for all stakeholders.

What is a market? A market is the place where goods and services are exposed for sale or exchanged for money. It can be physical or virtual. The virtual market place represents the Internet, which is increasingly becoming a force that is turning the whole world into a single market place. According to Bill Gates in his book *"Business at the Speed of Thought,"* "The Internet creates a new universal space for information sharing, collaboration, and commerce." The Internet is already revolutionizing the way business is conducted all over the world. Today the Internet provides nearly unlimited access to information about markets, products and competitors. Like never before a manufacturer in any geographical location has access to a wider global market. This implies that the business world will continue to be increasingly competitive and thanks to the appetite for the juicy investment opportunities Nigeria and the rest of Africa presents to foreign businesses. There are two implications of this, if a Nigerian business is doing well it can have access to a larger market than the immediate geographical location, but if a business delivers poorly it will definitely be wiped out by more aggressive oversea businesses!

LADEN WITH PRODUCTS

"And God blessed them, and God said unto them, Be fruitful, and multiply, and replenish the earth, subdue it: and have dominion over the fish of the sea, and over the fowl of the air, and over every living thing that moveth upon the earth."[42]

God created you, tested you, approved you as fit for production, and then he package you, and posted you on a divine assignment to Nigeria. Your mission to Nigeria is: bring forth products to meet the needs around you; mass produce that product; make sure it never finishes, by reproducing it and distributing it; take control of not only the market but also the economy with your product; and then rule your world by virtue of your control of the economy! Scientists have proven that no two humans on earth are the same. Since even identical twins have separate fingerprints. Everybody is unique; we all have unique products packaged into us waiting for release. There is a product in you that no other person carries; Nigeria and the whole world need that product.

SOLVING PROBLEMS

There is a need in Nigeria that you only can meet. There is a need in Africa that you were custom-built to meet. There are problems around you, that you were created to solve, there is a Goliath around you that you must kill if you must ascend your throne!

"For the earnest expectation of the creature waiteth for the manifestation of the Sons of God. For the creature was made subject to vanity, not willingly, but by reason of him who has subjected the same in hope, Because the creature itself also shall be delivered from the bondage of corruption into the glorious liberty of the children of God"[3]

Africans are waiting for you to provide the solution to their problems, are you going to deny them? All the things you complain about in Nigeria and Africa, health problems, poor electricity supply, dirty environments, unemployment, etc. are all waiting for you. I hope you will not disappoint destiny. God packaged the solution to all these problems into you when he created you, or else he won't send you to Africa!

"But we have this treasure in earthen vessels..."[2]

You need not look down on yourself. As small, as insignificant as you might think you are, there is something in you that the world needs. You can't afford to go to the grave with the treasure in you. You must release all that you carry so that you can die empty as much as possible. Appreciate the dignity and the worth of your personality, you have a treasure in you, a discovery of it will place you at the center of a big universe. You don't have to look like someone else. Even if the world does not believe in you (because all they can see is the ugly unattractive earthen vessel), believe in yourself, by the time you begin to meet their needs, they will change their minds! If you were created to solve a problem that's already solved, you won't be needed, and so God wouldn't have made you but there is a niche for you, there is a peculiar placement for you, you must discover it.

We need not envy the whites or citizens of any other nation, all they've done is to release their full worth, and we too can do the same. We need not wish we were Americans, or British, we can build a great nation as they have done. They've simply solved most of their basic problems and we too can solve our problems. They went further to create the institutions called Corporate America, which is responsible for the wealth creation in the US. All the companies in Corporate America were founded by individuals.

In 1863, John D. Rockefellers and his partners formed an oil business that eventually became the world's largest refining concern. Rockefellers founded in 1870, the standard Oil Company of Ohio the operations was later divided into 30 other corporations; which today include Exxon Mobil, Chevron and others. As a result Rockefellers was able to accumulate a personal fortune of $1billion, which is estimated to be 1.53% of the total U.S. annual GDP in his days. John D Rockefellers made several outstanding contributions to the US and the world through the Rockefellers foundation. His foundation pioneered the development of medical research and were instrumental in the eradication of hookworm and yellow fever. He was the founder of both the University of Chicago and Rockefeller University and funded the establishment of Central Philippine University in the Philippines.

Virtually in every industry there are men who have solved one problem or the other, and they consequently achieved phenomenal success. Talk about Henry ford in the automobile industry, Bill Gates in Computer Software, . All they did was to identify a need, created a product and subdued the earth with their product, and so they became the world's wealthiest!

Nigerians who are wishing or dreaming of the day they'll go to the US must ask themselves this question, why should I leave my prime location without releasing my product, and then go out there to celebrate someone else's product? Bill Gates released his product-Microsoft, when are you going to release your own product? Remember,

"The profit of the earth is for all: the king himself is served by the field."[6]

The profit of the earth is not only for Microsoft; it's also for you! Every celebrity on the earth today was served by the field, it wasn't luck. They had to cultivate their '*land*' to release their fruits or products. If you too can settle down to till your *'land'* you'll definitely bring forth a product that will help turn you into a global celebrity right on the soil of Nigeria!

"Much food is in the tillage of the poor: but there is that is destroyed for want of judgment"[44]

The above scripture means that wealth is potentially in every geographical location on the earth, and what brings out this wealth is a mental disposition to know the right step to take so as to unearth this wealth. The poorest countries in the world where not created poor by God, they became poor because they folded their hands and looking unto the distant lands not recognizing that all the wealth they will ever need is right in their backyard! They were opportunity blind!

CORPORATE WORLD

Corporations have enriched the societies that have embraced them, and there is no better gauge for the economic standard and the political freedom of a nation than the number of companies it harbors. There are several corporations in the US that are wealthier than many countries. For instance, Wal-Mart Stores Inc.'s (founded by Sam Walton) annual revenue for 2013 year ending was $469.162 billion[45], while the GDP of Nigeria in 2012 was $262.606 billion[9]. Hence, the company produces more economic value than the economy of Nigeria or South Africa!

The fact that the world's three richest men are worth more than the entire GDP of the world's 25 poorest countries, shows that these three guys creates more products and services than the 25 poorest countries put together! This should fuel a passion in every Nigerian. How can we be satisfied with having just three guys producing far more economic value than 170 million Nigerians!

Since *"there is no difference between the Jew and the Greek"*; you too can be the founder of a corporation right in Nigeria that will produce more economic value than the government of Nigeria! That's why you will never need to steal money from government to be rich. The economy of a nation cannot outgrow the economic power of the people of that nation. Why? As earlier mentioned, corporations founded by people are the ones that enriches a nation. So, instead of wishing you were in a nation with a big economy, become the big economic entity by creating products and services that meets the needs of the people where you are and the world over. After God made you and he said,

"…be fruitful, and multiply, and replenish the earth, and subdue it: and have dominion…" [42]

This means everyone created by God into Nigeria is a potentially great global economic entity! Every one created by God is potentially an institution. We can all create corporations.

Nigeria is where it is today because we are blind to the unique opportunities available for the creation of products and services to meet the needs around us. So, instead of meeting our own needs we turn to the west to help us meet them, hence making them wealthier, because the money flows from us to them.

When we recognize the needs around us and meet them by creating products and services, we'll be able to create global entities (corporations) that will continue to bring forth our products and services, long after we're gone from this world, just like the Fords, the Rockefellers, and the Walton.

We've heard of Ford, Mercedes, Apple, when are we going to hear about you? You, probably own a smartphone, say iPhone that means the American corporation has been able to convince you to buy their product, when are you going to convince the people of buying your own product? Or are you just going to pass through this world without releasing your product, while you continue to be a committed user of someone-else's product?

The world is filled today with people's products. A lot of us celebrate ourselves when we're able to acquire the means to buy into other people's product. We parade our nice watch, probably a swatch, we parade our nice cars probably a Mercedes, and also parade our nice houses, but, all these things are other people's product.

OFFERING A PRODUCT

Knowing fully well that *it is more blessed to give than to receive,* [45] you can only get blessed by what product you give your world. Start thinking seriously about the product and services you are going to leave behind, because you will only be remembered for what your product is. Robert Heller said unless your vision translates into a marketable product or service, it has no value. So, it is not enough to have vision or passion, you must turn your vision and passion into value.

"Give, and it shall be given unto you; good measure, pressed down, and shaken together, and running over, shall men give unto your bosom. For with the same measure ye mete withal it shall be measured back to you again."[46]

The law of giving and receiving states give a product and services to your world first, and the money will flow to you in the proportion of value added to the user of your product and services. Name one super rich guy, and you'll find out that his name is synonymous to a product and services. It's only in Nigeria that you'll see a rich guy that did not give anything, yet he has some money. How? He occupied a political post, and stole all the money that was entrusted to him! As I said earlier, that's the animal style! What product are you going to release?

"And the Lord God took the man, and put him into the Garden of Eden to dress it and to keep it. And the Lord commanded the man, saying, of every tree of the garden thou mayest freely eat:"[3]

And the Lord took you and put you into the Garden of Nigeria to dress and to keep it, and then your mouth will be satisfied by that garden you're keeping. There is a garden where you fit in the best; I mean there is a place where your product and services is most needed. Once you can locate that niche and the services that you're to supply, your food is eternally guaranteed!

Your primary assignment in Nigeria is to dress and keep Nigeria. You are to add value and beauty to both the environment and the lives of the people. Start by creating products and services for the emerging markets or innovative products for existing markets. Before you know it you will be fanning and kick-starting economic growth first for yourself and then for your nation.

In recent years most investors and businesses already know about the tremendous potential of Africa— the world's second-fastest-growing region, topped only by emerging Asia. But it may come as a surprise that Africa's growth is fuelled not by resources but rather by a rising consumer market. The continent's consumer-facing industries are expected to grow by $400 billion, representing its single-largest business opportunity, by 2020. This represent a huge opportunity for consumer focused products and services covering, apparel, financial services, groceries, the Internet, telecommunication and many more. This is the basis for the recent upsurge of multinational malls entrants into Nigerian market seeking to tap into the opportunities many Nigerians are oblivious of!

"Now will I sing to my well beloved a song of my beloved touching his vineyard. My well beloved hath a vineyard in a very fruitful hill: And he fenced it, and gathered out the stones thereof, and planted it with the choicest vine, and built a tower in the midst of it, and also made a wine press therein: and he looked that it should bring forth grapes, and it brought forth wild grapes. And now, O inhabitant of Jerusalem and men of Judah, judge I pray you, betwixt me and my vineyard. What could have been done more to my vineyard that I have not done in it? Wherefore when I looked that it should bring forth grapes, and it brought forth wild grapes? Now go to I will tell you what I will do to my vineyard: I will take away the edge thereof, and it shall be eaten up; and breakdown the wall thereof, and it shall be trodden down. And I will lay it waste..."[47]

God has done all he will ever do for us in Nigeria and Africa at large, he is so surprised at what is happening, he expects our economy to have advanced far more than where it is now. But when he comes around expecting to find all types of products and services, he finds poverty and unemployment, and he wonders is this the same Nigeria I endowed with so much human and natural resources. With the massive human resources of about 170 million people, God is expecting a huge economy, characterized by different types of products and services designed to meet the obvious needs in the country.

 From the above scripture, God is saying if we don't produce we are standing a risk of extinction! The poverty in Africa is due to lack of production of goods and services, because the forces of economy will not permit you to just exist without releasing a product! You either produce or you die economically! It's even the law of life to give out something or you die: the plants take in carbon dioxide and they give out oxygen; humans breathe in oxygen and breathe out carbon dioxide; in addition, we human take in carbohydrate from the plants and we give out feces which can serve as manure to the plants.

Staying alive hinges on this cycle of taking in and bringing out, any breakage in this cycle will terminate existence. You have bought a smartphone, you drive a car and so on, but may I ask you a question, when is your product coming into the market? We will never need to look up to any government to meet the needs around us because it is individuals God saddled with that responsibility. So, the question is what product and services are you going to offer your world?

"And there was a strife among them, which of them should be accounted the greatest.

And he said unto them, the king of the gentiles exercise lordship over them; and they that exercise authority over them are called benefactors. But ye shall not be so: but he that is greatest among you let him be as the younger; and he that is chief, as he that doth serve. For whether is greater, he that sitteth at meat, or he that serveth? Is not he that sitteth at meat? But I am among you as he that serveth."[39]

Jesus is saying wealth is guaranteed by being a producer and not a consumer. The richest man in the world is the man producing the most, and servicing the most people with his product. Don't focus on the goods and services you can buy, focus on the products and services you want to bring forth, because that's what will eventually determine your worth.

BRANDING

Brand is the name, term, design, symbol, or any other feature that identifies one seller's product distinct from those of other sellers. Initially it was used in the days of trade by barter to differentiate one person's cattle from another's, or one person's yam from another through a permanent mark on the product. Today. A brand is the most valuable asset of a corporation Every individual, every business every institution and every nation is a "brand": the sum total of the perceptions of all its customers, employees, suppliers, etc. Brands are living business assets, a concept, a feeling, a differentiating promise that grows, evolves, and will never die as long as a brand is kept alive in the minds of people. Branding is what you do to your business that makes every contact with your customer, suppliers and clients a memorable one making them choose you over and above the competition.

Over a decade ago, the financial times classed brands as the ultimate source of sustainable, competitive advantage. In 2011, the Economist stated that branded businesses enjoy margins double that of their counterparts, with greater levels of loyalty. In this increasingly competitive world, well managed brands, drive profits, hence businesses must employ a greater degree of innovation, sophistication, creativity, understanding and accountability. In today's competitive business landscape, two drivers of brand value are, choice (role of brand) and loyalty (brand strength). Purchase decision is increasingly becoming more fluid, but in order to win and sustain customer preference, a business must stay ahead of the competition in these two areas.

When you work on achieving brand excellence for your products and services, you will emerge the market leader. One of the greatest undoing of many Nigerian businesses is a disregard for excellence in delivery of product and services. This is why Nigerian products are synonymous with poor quality even among Nigerians how much more in the International market. You don't talk of branding, until achieve product quality and service excellence that can compete with the biggest global brands in the category. We have a long way to go in Nigeria. Our strategy must change from instant profit to long-term profit and sustainability. Your greatest competitive advantage is in achieving brand excellence- making your products and services the very best in the Industry.

"A man's gift maketh room for him, and bringeth him before great men."[48]
"Seest thou a man that is diligent in his business? He shall stand before kings; he shall not stand before mean men."[49]

Commitment to excellence is what creates a niche for you in the market place, making you the dominant force in the Industry. The quality of your product and services will determine your competitiveness in the global market palace. Note that the above scripture says the gift of a man and not the skin color of a man, or the location of a man.

What brings men in Corporate America to global prominence is nothing but their commitment to setting industry standards. Your gift talks about your uniqueness what you do the very best, what makes you different from the rest of the pack. When you concentrate on this, you can then establish a proprietary position that is based on being different and better.

It is time for us in the black world to become committed to excellence. It is time for us to personally erase our reproach from the eyes of the world by being committed to offering quality products and services at its peak, products that can rival any other in the global marketplace.

LOCATING THE PRODUCT WITHIN

"And the earth was without form, and void; and darkness was upon the face of the deep. And the Spirit of God move upon the face of the waters" [50]
"The spirit of man is the candle of the Lord, searching all inward parts of the belly" [51]
"But, there is a spirit in man: The inspiration of the Almighty giveth them understanding." [52]

To identify the products loaded into you by your creator you need to first sit down, and allow your spirit man to move searching all your inner being for the hidden product. That talks of thinking. The thinking room is the factory where products are released. The Spirit of God inspires an idea into you concerning the solution to a problem that has been bordering your heart, which in turn becomes your product and services.

"There is a man in thy kingdom, in whom is the spirit of the holy gods: and in the days of thy father light and understanding and wisdom, like the wisdom of the gods, was found in him; whom thy father masters of the magicians, astrologers, chaldeans, and soothsayers; For as much as an excellent spirit, and knowledge, and understanding, interpreting of dreams, and shewing hard sentences, and dissolving of doubts, were found in the same Daniel..."[53]

The solution to all types of hard problems can be made available to us when we engage the Holy Spirit in thinking through that problem. All the problems in Nigeria have solutions hidden in God, and as we engage the Holy Spirit in conscious thinking exercises he delivers them to us. There is a product to every problem in Nigeria, but that is only accessible to thinkers. All over the world thinkers have been known to be pacesetters. You can't release innovative products and services without thinking through.

Bill Gates the guy who created Microsoft was known to have started thinking as early as when he was in 6th grade, his mother called him over the intercom asking him why he hasn't come for dinner, he shouted back that he was thinking, his mother demanded, "thinking?" Bill responded, "Yes mom I'm thinking," he said fiercely. "Have you ever tried thinking" The result he has produced so far shows that he was actually thinking! Up till today Bill Gates still engages in qualitative thinking exercise. He has special holidays twice a year called, *'think week'* during which period he concentrates his thoughts on the most difficult technical and business problem facing his company, and recently he is focusing on global health issues. Little wonder he remains one of the richest Americans of all time.

New York Times asked Bishop David Oyedepo, "What do you do with your time?" he responded, "I think and I read!" The result he has produced so far with his life also shows that he thinks! It's time to go all out to release our full worth, by engaging in qualitative thinking exercises. Those 4 hours you spend on movies per day if you've been spending some of it thinking you would probably have been an employer of labor and not a job seeker!

4

STEWARDSHIP

"Moreover it is required in stewards, that a man be found faithful." Paul the Apostle

Stewardship is the art of keeping something in trust for another person. It is the art of keeping a thing that doesn't belong to you with the aim of making profit with that thing and then giving account of your dealings to the owner.

"The earth is the Lord and the fullness thereof; the world, and they that dwell therein."[54]

From above scripture, we understand that the whole world belong to God including Nigeria. Nigeria doesn't belong to the Government, or the different ethnic groups in it, Nigeria belongs to God. Both the human resources and the natural resources, and every other thing in the environment belong to God. The moment we begin to treat our nation, our environment, our institution and even fellow Nigerians as God's property, we'll increase our capacity for wealth.

VALUE

The value you place on something determines how well you'll keep that thing. The value you place on something will in turn determine the value that will accrue back to you. It's value for value. For instance, if a business place enough value on the customers and treat them with dignity and respect, the customer will in turn transfer some value to that business in form of more patronage, and more revenue. Sam Walton, the Founder of Wal-Mart Stores says, 'there is only one boss-the customer, and he can fire everybody in the company from the chairman on down, simply by spending his money somewhere else.' Little wonder the company remained one of the biggest company in the world in terms of revenue.

What determines the value you place on a thing is your understanding of the worth of that thing. A lot of us don't know our worth and the worth of fellow Nigerians, we don't know the worth of our environment, we don't know the worth of our resources, we don't know the worth of our time, we don't know the worth of our institutions and so we mismanage them.

God the owner of all things is watching how we Nigerians treat ourselves, our environment, resources, our institutions, and our time, and he is sad at what he is seeing. We have no value for human life, hence there has been no significant investment in healthcare, our so called tertiary health institutions are better as antiques, a far cry from the global trend in healthcare. We have no value for our resources; hence during ethnic clashes people can destroy petrol pipelines, set building on fire, and freely loot. Endemic with Nigerians is the embezzlement of public funds. We have zero value for our environment; hence Nigeria was globally known to have some of the dirtiest cities until recently. And even with the efforts of many state governments to clean up the cities, many people find it not convenient, and they criticize the change. We also have no value for our time, hence the concept of Nigerian time!

VALUE FOR HUMAN LIFE

Do we ever wonder why America is so blessed? We need not wonder, because these guys place value on themselves and on their country. America was called God's own country, by the founding fathers. They treated their resources, their environment, their institution and their fellow citizens as God's property. The value they placed on human life was reflected in those majestic words of the declaration of independence:

"We hold these truths to be self-evident, that all men are created equal, that they are endowed by God, Creator, with certain inalienable Rights, that among these are Life, Liberty, and the pursuit of Happiness." [15]

Notice the universalism of the above statement. It doesn't say "some men"; it says "all men.", which means that all men have basic rights that are neither derived from nor conferred by the state. The founding fathers were influenced by the Bible. They understand the concept of the image of God, which is the idea that all men have something within them that God injected. Bringing this idea closer home, all Nigerians are made in the image of God and so they have something in them that God injected, that's the life of God. If we understand this we won't treat ourselves like animals, but rather with dignity and respect like we would treat God!

"Jesus said unto him, Thou shalt love the Lord thy God with all thy heart, and with all thy soul, and with all thy mind. This is the first commandment. And the second is like unto it, thou shall love thy neighbour as thyself. On these two commandments hang all the law and the prophets." [55]

"If a man says I love God and hate his brother, he is a liar: for he that loveth not his brother whom he hath seen, how can he love God whom he hath not seen?"[56]

There is no gradation between the love for God, for you and for fellow Nigerians. All the principle of success and wealth, hinges on love and the placement of the right value on all humans. When we Nigerians begin to value ourselves as we would value God, our creativity opens, because we will aim at adding value to each other. Customer loyalty cannot be bought; it is earned through commitment to customer needs. There cannot be genuine financial success without value for one another.

The man offering substandard products and services so as to maximize profit is minimizing his profit unknowingly. He is invariably limiting his business coast, because excellence is what brings your products and services to the fore fronts in the global market place. The man who's fond of shouting at and insulting his customers will soon go out of business. The moment we have the right value for the life of Nigerians we'll offer services that treats customers as kings and queens, and that is the key to business success.

STEWARDSHIP OF OUR ENVIRONMENT

"And the Lord took the man, and put him into the Garden of Eden to dress and to keep it."[3]

God placed us into the garden of Nigeria to keep and to dress it. That talks about making our environment safe, secure, clean and beautiful. Our primary responsibility as stewards of God's earth is to keep it clean, beautiful, and free from all pollutants. How does this apply to business? If we Nigerians can keep our environment clean, beautiful and secure don't you think we will be able to grow our tourism industry? Our weather is all year-round summer, which is what the whites love and spend billions of dollars on yearly. But our undoing is that we've not taken time to invest in our environment.

"And the Lord planted a garden eastward in Eden; and there he put the man whom he has formed."[3]

If God had to invest before Eden was birthed, we too must invest in our environment to make it beautiful. Globally, the tourism industry is a multibillion-dollar industry but Nigeria is not yet a player. There are countries on earth today where tourism provides a good portion of their foreign exchange. Malaysians tourism industry account for 28% of their employment, which is one of the basis for their transformation from a producer of raw materials to an emerging multi-sector economy.[57] Today the Nigerian tourism industry is untapped; this signifies a unique opportunity for savvy entrepreneurs.

STEWARDSHIP OF OUR RESOURCES

"He said therefore, a certain nobleman man went into a far country to receive for himself a kingdom, and to return. And he called the ten servants and delivered them ten pounds, and said unto them, occupy till I come...And it came to pass, that when he was returned, having received the kingdom, then he commanded these servants to be called unto him, to whom he whom he had given the money, that he might know how much every man had gained by trading. Then came the first, saying Lord, thy pound hath gained ten pounds. And he said unto him, well, thou good servant: because thou hath been faithful in a very little, have thou authority over ten cities. And the second came, saying, Lord, thy pound hath gained five pounds. And he said likewise to him, be thou also over five cities. And another came, saying, Lord, behold here is thy pound, which I have kept laid up in a napkin: For I fear thee, because thou art an austere man: thou takest up that thou ladest not down, and reapest that thou did not sow. And he said unto him out of thine own mouth will I judge thee, thou wicked servant. Thou knowest that I am an austere man, taking up that I lay not down, and reaping that I did not sow: Wherefore then gavest not thou my money into the bank, that at my coming I might have required my own with usury? And he said unto them that stood by, take from him the pound, and give unto him that hath ten pounds. And they said unto him, Lord he hath ten pounds. For I say unto you, that upon every one which hath shall be given; and from him that hath not, even that he hath shall be taken away from him."[58]

This episode reveals the following about how God views our resources especially our money:

> ➤ The money in our hands and the one in our bank accounts were given to us by God in trust, it is not our money, and neither does it belong to the government! Remember, *"The silver and the gold are mine...*"[59]*So* he demands high-level accountability from us.
>
> ➤ God expects us to do business with the money and the resources he has entrusted into our hands.
>
> ➤ God expects us to make profit by investing his money within a specific time frame after which he will demand our financial statement. I mean God is profit oriented.
>
> ➤ From ten pounds to ten cities shows that by being a faithful

steward of money, an individual, a business or an institution will enjoy a phenomenal level of increase and expansion! So the problem is not that any body was born poor, the problem is that they remained poor by not been astute investors of God's money! Remember, *"He becometh poor that dealeth with a slack hand..."*[60]

➤ God will punish all those who couldn't cause his money to increase for whatever reason.

➤ If there was distribution of the money on earth equally among every nation and people, and you come back after a specified time frame, the money would have redistributed itself, returning to the original state before distribution.

➤ Money tends to migrate from poor managers to concentrate with expert managers!

From these lessons, we can draw that the poorest people, the poorest businesses and the poorest nations are those that ignore the importance of money and naively claim they don't need to learn about it while the wealthiest people, businesses and nations are those men who handle the investment of their money and resources astutely. What determines the financial future of any person, any business, and any institution is not the volume of money on ground but how they manage what's on ground. Your business can grow from revenue of $10 to become an economic entity controlling the economy of ten cities, ten states and ten countries! All you need do is to be accountable wherever you are financially, because you can't outgrow your level of financial accountability! For a business to grow from $10 to that of controlling ten cities, its finance must have been handled as though it were a big corporate organization, even when it was just a small shop! God does not waste his resources, he tries you on small, before he allows you to enlarge. Everybody was at one time small and it has been said that more than 90% of financially successful people started off broke.

"Another parable put the forth unto them, saying, the kingdom of heaven is like to a grain of mustard seed, which a man took and sow in his field: Which indeed is the least of all seeds: but when it is grown, it is the greatest among herbs, and becometh a tree, so that the birds of the air come and lodge in the branches thereof."[61]

Any man who understands how to manage money in terms of investment and accountability can grow from the poorest to the wealthiest! So, the problem is not that you are indeed the least of all men; the problem is that you don't understand that what's in your hand is the seed that links you to the great future you have seen. Anybody can become anything, all they need do is to understand the times and season of life.

"To everything there is a season and a time to every purpose under the heaven: A time to be born and a time to die; a time to plant, and a time to pluck that which is planted…"[62]

You don't receive a return on investment immediately. It takes time. In the same way it takes time to grow from $10 to ten cities! If you don't appreciate this timing you will not be able to discipline yourself in your spending. You must be humble enough to appreciate that *life is in phases and men are in sizes*. This will help you to live your size per time, or else you will end up eating your seed and your future! Name any man who has attained some level of genuine financial success; they are usually great stewards of money. Bill Gates, the founder of Microsoft and Co-chairman of Bill and Melinda Gates Foundation has a rule that Microsoft instead of incurring debt must always have enough money in the bank to run for a year even with no revenues! Little wonder Microsoft remained one of the most highly valued companies in the world even after Gates left active participation in the company. But you, both your capital and your profit goes straight to your stomach, no wonder your business can't last more than a day with no revenue!

"Praise ye the Lord, blessed is the man that fearest the Lord…Wealth and riches shall be in his house: and his righteousness endureth forever…A good man showeth favor, and lendeth: he will guide his affairs with discretion."[63]

The reason why despite the fact that wealth and riches are in this guy's house, he still had to guide his affairs with discretion was because that was how the money came in the first place and so to keep it there he must be disciplined in his spending. Those who cannot be disciplined in their spending cannot be rich, because:

"He that loveth pleasure shall be a poor man: he that loveth wine and oil shall not be rich."[64]

Some people claim shopping is their hobby, some others say their hobby is to buy the latest cars, but to a savvy investor like Warren Buffet, their hobby equals wasting of money. Buffet, the 4th wealthiest person in the world has an investment strategy that mirrors his lifestyle and overall philosophy for life: he doesn't live in a huge house, he doesn't collect cars, and he doesn't take a limousine to work. In fact, "The Oracle of Omaha" lives in the same house he once bought for $31,500. Even a quick look at Berkshire Hathaway's (His Company) website would never tell you that the company is worth over $200 Billion. Is it bad to live in a huge house or is it bad to drive a limousine? No! This guy is simply operating a philosophy that makes wealth easy. But some of us our greatest barrier to wealth is a lifestyle of waste. Same is true of our great nation Nigeria, where corruption has eaten into every fabrics of the society resulting in hyper inflated cost of developmental projects and governance. As a matter of fact, this is most people's hidden reason for going into politics; so that they can share in the 'loot'. No wonder wealth has eluded us in this part of the world! There is no short cut; you can never see wealth and waste inhabit the same place!

"When Jesus lifted up his eyes, and saw a great company come unto him, he saith unto Philip, Whence shall we buy bread that these may eat? And this he said to prove him for he himself knew what he would do…And Jesus said, make the men sit down. Now there was much grass in the place. So the men sat down in number about five thousand. And Jesus took the loaves; and when he had given thanks, he distributed to the disciples, and the disciples to them that were set down; and likewise of the fishes as much as they would. When they were filled, he said unto his disciples, gather up the fragments that remain, that nothing be lost. Therefore they gathered them together, and filled twelve baskets with the fragments of the five barley loaves, which remain over and above unto them that had eaten."[65]

Can you imagine a guy who had enough money to be asking for where they'll buy food to feed five thousand men, yet ordering his boys to gather up the fragments and crumbs so that nothing will be wasted! Wealth is indeed not a friend of waste! Jesus would have just left the remaining fragments to waste, and then when next they need some food he would perform another miracle, but that is not how God operates. He believes in maximizing what's on ground, before he releases another to prevent waste. If you don't maximally utilize the resources God has placed around you now, you won't graduate to a higher level of wealth.

STEWARDSHIP OF OUR TIME

"My times are in thy hand…"[66]

We neither own time nor control time; God is the owner and the controller. Time is the break in eternity that permits us humans to fulfill destiny.

"And we know that all things work together for good to them that love God, to them who are called according to his purpose. For whom he did foreknow, he did also predestinate to be conformed to the image of his Son that he might be first born among many brethren."

Before the beginning began, before you were created, before time began, God decided what assignment you are to perform on earth and then gave you the time so that you can fulfill that assignment. Time can be said to be God's permission away from eternity to allow the accomplishment of a particular mission. The only reason God gave time is for the fulfillment of man's purpose.

"To everything there is a season, and a time to every purpose under the heaven: A time to be born, and a time to die; a time to plant, and a time to pluck up that which is planted;"[62]

Our time as individuals began the moment we were born that means God having concluded what mission we were to accomplish, allowed us to be brought forth to accomplish that mission. That means from the day we were born God began marking the time, with every tick of the clock God is counting, and thinking, "I hope this guy will hit the target I have set before him." So, stewardship of time begins with an understanding that we are here on earth on a divine assignment plus a discovery of that assignment. Stewardship of time begins with having a vision and a dream in life, or having a set target for one's life.

"He hath made everything beautiful in his time: also he hath set the world in their heart…"[63]

He hath set the world in their heart is also translated, "he has set eternity in their heart." Everyman has the ability to make a discovery of their purpose; their essence of being, and the value they are designed to add to their world. When we engage in deep thinking; a retrospective trip into our hearts, we will always catch a glimpse of the products and services we are designed to deliver to our world.. Once we have the idea of our mission we can then begin a journey of fulfillment. The journey is enhanced only by making use of a timetable, because to every mission there is a time frame required for its accomplishment.

Time is a portion of eternity allocated for the accomplishment of a mission. This therefore means that the only thing a faithful steward of God's time will do with time is to be pursuing his assignment within God's timetable. Jesus the most accomplished man who ever lived is the man who understand time the most, as evidence by such statements as *"my time is not yet."* Jesus knew that every assignment has a timetable within which it is performed. When the concept of timing is understood we'll realize that it is not our time, it is his time and all assignments yields good result when they are performed within his timetable.

God gives the ultimate vision or mission statement for our lives and the overall time required for its accomplishment, but it is our responsibility to plan our time, breaking the overall goal into short-term goals allocating a specific time frame for their accomplishment.

"See that ye walk circumspectly, not as fools but as wise, redeeming the time because the days are evil."[69]
"Surely goodness and mercy shall follow me all the days of my life…"[70]

In the same way Christ redeem us from the curse of the law, so that the blessing of Abraham may come upon us the gentiles, God expects us to redeem our time and free ourselves from the evil each day has an ability of bringing. We redeem our time by walking circumspectly, meaning we take all our actions and decision in a particular day only after careful thought about our mission in life. When we take only well planned actions –actions that links with our mission, we will be able to enjoy goodness. To redeem also means to get the money worth of something, so, when we plan our time to link up with our mission by the hour, days, weeks, months and years, and take only actions that are in the plan, we would have freed ourselves from the evil in that day and subsequently enjoy the full money worth of that day. It is only after doing this that times becomes money.

There are guys on earth today who have invested their times so much so that the amount of money they make by the hour, day, week and year is mind-blowing! For instance as at January 1997, Bill Gates was making about $30 million a day![71] That means this guy was making more than a million dollar per hour! Sure that's more than what a lot of people will make in a lifetime! But remember he started thinking through his action since he was a small boy. If we Nigerians can embrace the concept of investing time and not spending or wasting it, we'll surely enter this realm of goodness. May I say this, what we earn now in Nigeria per hour, per day, per week, per month is a reflection of the level of investment we have done with our time in the past! Remember the Nigerian time concept? The value you place on your time will determine the value that time will accrue back to you. Value is the amount of money that something is worth. The value you place on your time today will determine your net worth in the future! Bill Gates is worth several billion dollars today, how much are you going to be worth in the future? Remember,

"The profit of the earth is for all: the king himself is served by the fields."[6]

STEWARDSHIP TO PRINCIPLES

According to Steven R. Covey, Principles are guidelines for human conduct that are proven to have enduring permanent value. They are fundamental. They are essentially unarguable because they are self-evident. Just as there are natural laws such as gravity which govern the physical dimension, principles are natural laws which govern the human dimension. Principles are so paramount to human existence that the extent to which people in society recognize and live in harmony with them moves them toward either survival and stability, or disintegration and destruction!

Principles refer to values, ethics and code of conducts. You can't just do anything, live anyhow and expect to arrive at a place of prominence. The fact that you've never heard people talk about how desirable an accident was shows that no admirable thing happens by accident. Stop expecting to reap what you have not sown. If your goal is to harvest tomorrow, then you must invest today. The whole of life is a conscious adventure. You have to consciously discipline your life to adhere to principles. You have to consciously subscribe to the pains, so as to enjoy the gains! There are two pains in life, the pains of discipline and the pains of regret. The pains of discipline weighs ounces while that of regret weighs pounds! Why should you wake up at the age of 75 years and discover that your life would have had more color if you had played by the rules! You can move your life from mere existence to great significance by adhering to principles. The higher you want to go in life, the deeper you must root yourself into eternal principles.

Instant gratification is a shortcut to instant crucifixion! If you arrive at a place of prominence by evading eternal principles you are simply setting the stage for a disastrous and shameful fall. Remember that the first man, Adam, was the CEO of Eden, one of the most admirable corporations that ever existed, but he had a shameful exit when he evaded eternal principles. It doesn't matter the size of your empire, it can disappear overnight if you keep evading principles. Check out how the scandals in Corporate America wiped out formidable companies like Enron and Arthur Andersen, leaving their top execs with jail terms. It's okay to ignore values if you don't want to amount to much in life, but if you want to emerge as a global celebrity, you must root your life in values and character. A wise man said, "Charisma can take you to the top, but it takes character to maintain you at the top." Character is the foundation for lasting success.

"Righteousness exalteth a nation: but sin is a reproach to any people." [72]

Individuals, organizations and societies that ignore and evade principles have been known to fail over time and disintegrate or better still go into extinction. To evade values is to self-destruct! How can you explain the slow economic growth of African countries and the rapid accelerated growth of South-East Asian Countries? Consider that in 1965 Nigeria's GDP was almost as much as that of Malaysia and Indonesia puts together. By 1995 Malaysia had a 27 fold increase in GDP, Indonesia a 52 fold increase, and Nigeria a miserable 3.6 fold. The Malaysians who were targeting catching up with Nigeria level GDP by the end of the 1980s had an economy in nominal GDP per capital terms that was more than 10 times that of Nigeria at the time of the Asian financial crisis in 1997.

There may be many factors to explain the above disparity between Nigeria and East Asian countries, but a singular factor that is more pronounced in Nigeria compared with these countries is corruption. Don't be surprised when you check out the list of the most corrupt countries in the world and it coincides with the poorest and least developed countries! That is simply the principle. Individuals, organizations and nations that evade principles always end up in a life of reproach and shame. Well, what has happened has happened, we cannot change the past, but we can deliberately and consciously choose our future, by subscribing to the demands of a principled life as a national motto.

5

ENTREPRENEURSHIP

"Teaching someone to spend his life working for earned income is like teaching him to be a high paid slave for life."_Robert Kiyosarki

An entrepreneur is someone who starts a company, arranges business deals, and takes risks in order to make profit. An entrepreneur is a person who capitalizes on unmet needs of people to build a business system that will service those needs with a goal of making profit for all stakeholders. Entrepreneurship therefore is the art of capitalizing on unmet needs of people to create a business system to service those needs with the aim of making profit for all stakeholders. A business is someone's solution to a problem, so entrepreneurs are solution providers.

The world's richest men became rich not by working for money but by making money. Real wealth is not earned in form of a salary but rather it is created. The fact that 60% of Nigerians live below the poverty line (live on less than $1 a day) is a proof that we're not using our God given creative abilities to create wealth. It is so pathetic to watch the way we criticize our government as if they are the reason for our predicaments. We claim that the government is not creating enough jobs as if it is the responsibility of the government to do that. I personally feel there is something about paid employment that makes one complacent resulting in stiffening of creativity! Some employees are nothing but high paid slaves because their creativity is for the benefit of their employers! I believe there is no job that can pay you as much as your gift can pay you.

Mr. Joseph was an employee of Potiphar the Chief of Staff in Ancient Egypt and he was enjoying the job with rapid promotion and benefits. Within no time Joseph became the CEO of Potiphar's business. But one day, because he wasn't ready to compromise his values a conspiracy against him cost him his high paying job and his freedom. He was locked up in a maximum security prison. Everybody thought his case was closed. But his gift of interpreting dreams made room for him in the palace. He solved a national problem and he became the Prime Minister in the same Egypt! How about his formal boss? I guess he remained the Chief of Staff while Joseph became his boss!

That you don't have a job now or that you've just lost your formal job is not new! As a matter of fact it is an opportunity in disguise for you! Mr. Joseph would never have risen above his boss had it been that he didn't lose his job. You have a deposit of treasure in you capable of taking you to global prominence, why should you die as a high paid slave!

"A good man leaveth an inheritance to his children's children"[80]

The above scripture shows that God's expectation of us is to have enough wealth that will transcend our third generation. No matter how high paying your job may be you're not likely to be able to accumulate that kind of wealth. As we said earlier real wealth is created. How do you create wealth? Wealth creation starts by your discovery of your gift and then matching it with a need. Every gift in every human meets a particular need. A manufacturer does not make a product without a well-defined use. It was a need on the earth- precisely Nigeria that necessitated your creation by God. To claim you're unemployed is a sign of mental laziness! As a matter of fact the only people permitted to be unemployed are those who cannot coordinate mental activities! You've got to first sit down to discover your gift, your skill, and your uniqueness and then match it with a need or a problem in Nigeria. Unemployment, which means absence of a job, is an opportunity for you to look inward so that you can release your treasure to the world.

NEEDS OF PEOPLE

Abraham Maslow (1954) was a social psychologist that provided explanation for the types of priority needs which individuals requires and is found necessary throughout life. These are the things required for not only staying alive but for living an enhanced standard of life. Maslow identified 5 types of needs found to be common for all human beings irrespective of cultural background. In order of ascendance, the needs are:

- ➤ Physiological Needs: These are required for nourishment, growth and development. These include good food, water, and health care.
- ➤ Safety Needs: Required for protection and prevention from injury to the individual so that survival can be guaranteed. These include shelter and security of lives and property.
- ➤ Love and Belonging: Required for sustainability of emotional state of the individual, hence mental health. Include man's need for love, friendly relationships at all levels.
- ➤ Self Esteem: Required for repetition of desired and beneficial

action by and for the individual. Required to keep the individual wanting to achieve greater success and excellence. This talks about man's desire to be up-front, to surpass others, to achieve distinction, to lead the parade, to stay ahead of the rest of the pack.

➤ Self-Actualization: Required to signify a level of satisfaction, hence the desired gratification from a pursuit and accomplishment. It is the peak of all expectation and largely subjective.

Note that there is no mention of man's need for money. Money is not part of the basic needs of life; money is just a means to an end. Remember that long ago people even traded without money. They called it trade by barter, which is the process of exchanging what you have for what you need. Mike Murdock said money is nothing but a reward for service.

"And unto one he gave five talents, to another two, and to another one, to every man according to their several abilities, and straight way took his journey. Then he that had received the five talents went and traded with the same, and made them other five talents." 81

Everybody has a gift, treasure, skill that they can trade for what they need. There is something in you that your world needs, if you must have money then you've got to learn how to trade with what you have. If you think you have nothing then you've got to learn a skill, or develop a talent that you can trade with. The reason we all go to school is to develop skills that are marketable- a skill that will help us meet a need in our world. When you meet the needs around you with your skill, talent, product and services, the money will flow to you. To claim you can't make genuine money in Nigeria is to be blind! Now hear this, the only country in the world where you can't make money is that in which there are no needs. Since all humans have needs, the only country in which you can't make money is that in which there are no people! Nigeria's huge population is sure a huge market for any man to tap into in any industry.

Imagine the huge market for good, affordable, hygienic food created by our huge population. In this market the supply must be enormous to meet the demand. The largely subsistence agricultural sector has failed to keep up with the rapid population growth, and Nigeria, once a large net exporter of food, now must import food. There is an obvious need for innovative entrepreneurs in the food industry in Nigeria: production (agricultural or industrial), processing, packaging, distribution and retailing. The world is looking eagerly at Africa as the continent with the largest undeveloped arable land resource in the world. The call therefore goes out to Nigerian entrepreneurs to wake up to the opportunities that agribusiness sector has to offer and not to wait for companies from elsewhere to walk away with the spoil.

How about in the healthcare industry? The fact that majority of the health care providers in Nigeria are government employees shows a lack of entrepreneurial skill. There is an obvious demand for world class health care delivery. The percentage of government expenditure on health care was about 1.5% in the early 1990s, though this meager amount has grown to about 4.5% in 2012, this is still a far cry from the WHO recommendation of 15%. Today, Nigeria's healthcare system is woefully underfunded and grossly ineffective, accounting for some of the worst health indices in the world. There is a huge need for world class healthcare delivery that can compete with any in the world. This creates an opportunity for business savvy healthcare entrepreneurs to fill the great vacuum created by this need.

How about safety needs? The need for good, quality, safe and affordable housing for the vast population of Nigerians residing in very poor accommodation is obviously a huge business opportunity. The 17 million housing deficit in Nigeria means a huge opportunity for low cost world class housing infrastructure. There is obviously a huge demand in Nigeria for holiday resorts, recreation centres and parks where people can develop friendship, and build their various types of relationships and of course build the tourism industry. How about the individual needs for achieving greater success and excellence? Education of this vast population is one major strategy to meet this need. In 2001, 763,057 students sat for UME while the total admission for that year was only 50,277. This means that the over 50 universities in Nigeria are meeting only 6.6% of the university education needs! This signifies a huge opportunity for private universities. There are other innovative educational products and services that will meet the huge individual needs for achieving success and excellence.

"And God gave Solomon wisdom and understanding exceeding much, and largeness of heart, even as the sand that is on the sea shore. And Solomon's wisdom excelled the wisdom of all the children of the east country, and all the wisdom of Egypt. For he was wiser than all men…And he spake three thousand proverbs: and his songs were a thousand and five…And there came of all people to hear the Wisdom of Solomon, from all kings of the earth, which had heard of his wisdom."[82]
"So King Solomon exceeded all the kings of the earth for riches and for wisdom. And all the earth sought to Solomon to hear his wisdom, which God had put in his heart. And they brought every man his present, vessels of silver, and vessels of gold, and garments, and amour, and spices, horses, and mules, a rate year by year."[83]

Solomon devised a means to convert the gift God gave him into innovative wisdom products that would service the needs of everybody on earth at that time. Little wonder he became the richest man in his world because the world paid him year by year for the service rendered. Imagine a guy servicing 7 billion people on earth with innovative wisdom products and services! He obviously had a website which the world could visit to log on to his numerous services at a price per annum. There are many innovative products we can offer to our world. Innovation is the process of translating vision into marketable products or services to create value for an anticipated customer demand and thus initiating trends rather than following it. The intense competitive business environment in today's world makes it a must for any entrepreneur that wants to stay ahead of the rest of the pack to keep innovating.

What an entrepreneur does is to create a business solution to the problems around and help improve the quality of life of the masses with his innovation. We must not leave our problems in the hands of the foreign investors to solve, because when they do, they usually repatriate their income for the development of their home country, since they have no vested interest in the development of Nigeria. When I see a foreigner in Nigeria, I am always convinced that these guys are here to explore the opportunities we Nigerians have left untapped. Imagine what we do, we lament that the Lebanese, Indian or Chinese companies are paying us poorly for our labor. Who said we cannot employ them instead? This is a mind problem! The opportunities in Nigeria are so huge that foreigners don't mind staying in the harsh business environment as compared to their home country in order to make some profit.

STARTING A SMALL BUSINESS

Starting small is important to overcome the inertial of starting. But you don't have to remain small. As a matter of fact you've got to start with a big dream because no business will ever outgrow its founding vision. You start with your eyes focused on your big dream, but your hand on the place where you are working out the way to the future. Starting small helps you to prove the profitability of your business model, while at the same time minimizing the risk. It's better to prove the profitability of your business model before seeking investors, because investors only put their money where there is guaranteed returns on investment.

Starting and managing a business takes motivation, desire and talent. It also takes research and planning. Like a chess game, success in small business starts with decisive and correct opening moves. To increase your chance of success, take the time up front to explore your personal and business goals. Then use this information to build a comprehensive and well-thought out business plan that will help you reach these goals.

"An enterprise is built by wise planning, becomes strong through common sense and profit wonderfully by keeping abreast of the facts."[84]

Building a successful enterprise requires a lot of planning, and research in order to get the relevant facts about the business environment, the competition, the customers, opportunities and general overview of the market. The process of developing a business plan will help you think through some important issues that you may not have considered yet. Your plan will become a valuable tool as you set out to raise money for your business. It should also provide milestones to gauge your success.

GETTING STARTED

Before starting out, list out your reasons for wanting to go into business.

Next you need to determine what is "right for you." Ask yourself these questions:
> ➢ What do I like to do with my time?
> ➢ What skill have I learned or developed?
> ➢ What do others say I am good at?
> ➢ How much time do I have to run a successful business?
> ➢ Do I have any hobbies or interests that are marketable?

Then you should identify the niche your business will fill. Conduct the necessary research to answer these questions:
> ➢ Is my idea practical and will it fill a need?
> ➢ What is my competition?
> ➢ What is my business advantage over existing firms?
> ➢ Can I deliver a better quality service?
> ➢ Can I create a demand for my business?

The final step before developing your plan is the pre-business checklist. You should answer these questions:
> ➢ What business am I interested in starting?
> ➢ What services or products will I sell? Where will I be located?
> ➢ What skill and experience do I bring to the business?

> What will be my legal structure?
> What will I name my business?
> What equipment or supplies will I need?
> What insurance coverage will be needed?
> What financing will be needed?
> What are my resources?
> How will I compensate myself?

Your answers will help you create focused, well-researched business plan that should serve as a blueprint. It should detail how the business will be operated, managed and capitalized.

BUSINESS STRUCTURE

The way successful entrepreneurs compete with big companies with more money and more people is by creating great teams. An entrepreneur sees an opportunity, puts together a team, and builds a business that profit from the opportunity. An entrepreneur must be able to pull together smart people from different disciplines and skills and have them work together to achieve a common goal. The better you can lead a team of smart qualified people, without having to work as a member of the team, the bigger and better entrepreneur you can become. The business structure includes:
> The entrepreneur
> The investor(s)
> The specialists: Depending on the type of business being formed, specialist usually includes the professionals like accountants, lawyers, doctors, engineers, computer scientists, surveyors and so on.
> The employees

Factors influencing your decision about your business structure include:
> Legal restrictions
> Liabilities assumed
> Types of business operation
> Earnings distribution
> Capital needs
> Number of employees
> Tax issues
> Length of business operation

It's pertinent to note the value of developing a sound business structure.

You are not likely to secure quality investors without a sound business structure in place. Today, companies in Africa can access sophisticated strategic advice and wide array of investors' capital that historically has only been available to the world largest companies. Private capital is increasingly penetrating the African market and is expected to continue to grow, because the GDP rates for the continent continues to grow at rates greater than the mature economies of Europe and North America. A sound professional business structure in place will help your company secure access to world class sophisticated capital.

THE BUSINESS PLAN

A business plan precisely defines your business, identifies your goals and serves as your firm's résumé. The basic components include a current and pro forma balance sheet, an income statement, and cash flow analysis. It helps you allocate resources properly, handle unforeseen complications, and make good business decisions. Because it provides specific and organized information about your company and how you will repay invested money, a good business plan is crucial part of any capital raising endeavor. It is what will either ward off or commit a potential investor to your business. It is what the globally minded institutional investors will require for you to qualify for their private capital.

Introduction:

- ➢ Give a detail description of the business and its goals. This should include the mission statement of the business. Stephen R Covey has this to say of mission statement: "One of the most powerful methods to cultivate the passion of vision is to create and live by a mission statement, philosophy, or creed. Such statements capture what you want to do-what qualities you want to develop, what you want to accomplish, what contributions you want to make. Clarity on these issues is critical because it affects everything else-the goals you set, the decisions you make, the paradigm you hold, and the way you spend your time."
- ➢ Discuss the ownership of the business and the legal structure.
- ➢ List the skill and experience you bring to the business
- ➢ Discuss the advantages you and your business have over your competitor.

Marketing:

- ➢ Discuss the products and services offered.

- Identify the customer demand for your product and service.
- Identify your market, its size and locations.
- Explain how your product and service will be advertised and marketed.
- Explain strategy, the pricing strategy.

Financial Management:

- Explain your source and the amount of initial equity capital.
- Develop a monthly operating budget for the first year.
- Develop an expected return on investment and monthly cash flow for the first year.
- Provide projected income statements and balance sheets for a two year period.
- Discuss your breakeven point.
- Explain your personal balance sheet and method of compensation.
- Explain who will maintain your accounting records and how they will be kept.
- Provide "what if" statement that addresses alternative approaches to any problem that may develop.

Operations:

- Explain how the business will be managed on day-to-day basis.
- Discuss hiring and personnel procedures.
- Discuss insurance, lease or rent agreements, and issues pertinent to your business.
- Account for the equipment necessary to produce your products or services.
- Account for production and delivery of products and services.

Concluding Statement:

- Summarize your business goals and objectives and express your commitment to the success of your business.
- Once you have completed your business plan, review it with a friend or business associate.
- When you feel comfortable with the content and the structure make an appointment to review and discuss it with your investor, your banker or your lender. The business plan is a flexible document that should change as your business grows.

No matter the business you are starting, it is very important to put in place the structures above, if you must tap into the opportunities in Nigeria. Businesses that cannot run itself are those that have no structure in place. What differentiate a self-employed from a business man is that a self-employed man works for himself, while a business man creates teams and built structures around those teams to solve problems while creating profit for all stakeholders. What investors invest in are teams that have a track record of solving problems and creating profit over time.

6

SUSTAINABLE DEVELOPMENT

Sustainability is the capacity to endure. In ecology the word describes how biological systems remain diverse and productive over a long time. Long-lived and healthy wetlands and forests are examples of sustainable biological systems. For humans, sustainability is the potential for long-term maintenance of well-being, which has ecological, economic, political and cultural dimensions. Sustainability requires the reconciliation of environmental, social equity and economic demands.

Sustainable development, according to Brundtland Commission is development that meets the needs of the present without compromising the ability of the future generations to meet their needs. Sustainable development is development that improves the quality of human life while promoting and enhancing the carrying capacity of the supporting eco-system today and in the future. This means putting into consideration economic equity for social and economic inclusion, political inclusion and environmental sustainability. Sustainability ensures we are able to tackle future challenges so that we can make positive contribution to our society in the present whilst also ensuring that the generation yet unborn are better off than the present.

ENVIRONMENTAL SUSTAINABILITY

Environmental sustainability is the ability of the environment to meet the basic requirements for the sustenance of the living and the non-living components of the ecological, economic and socio-cultural systems in a manner that does not limit the possibility of meeting the present and the future needs. What will be the effect of the unchecked deforestation, continuous gas flaring and pollution of the fresh water on the next generation of Nigerians. One of the reasons many of us love traveling overseas is to enjoy the green lurch vegetation and freshness of the air, water ways and environment of the countries we visit. While it is not bad to visit other countries, it is bad and appalling to leave our own environment degraded, whilst we settle abroad contributing to the sustenance of those environment.

Every environment is planted and nurtured by someone, the lush garden of White House or the mountainous green scenery of Switzerland didn't drop from heaven, rather it was planted and nurtured by some fellows. Even God, had to plant the Garden of Eden, and he placed the responsibility of dressing it on the man he made.

"And the Lord planted a garden eastward in Eden; and there he put the man whom he has formed." [3]

Every Nigerian has a responsibility to keep the and dress the Nigerian environment. We don't need to envy any nation for their environment, or wish we were born in those environment, neither do we need to blame our government. We are all responsible for the environmental degradation Nigeria has suffered. We are the only one that can rewrite the environmental story of Nigeria. All we need to do is to plant our own garden and keep it lush and green.

"Look not upon me, because I am black, because the sun hath looked upon me: my mother's children were angry with me; they made me the keeper of the vineyards but mine own vineyard have I not kept." [86]

What makes you black and inferior is not your skin color, but your mindset, resulting in your preference to keep the garden of others, whilst your home garden is brown and unkempt. When you fail to keep the garden placed in your care, you surfer shame and reproach like the man in the above scriptures. Our total disregard for the ecosystem we live in is a subtle way to self-destruct. We are simply preparing a racial extinction for our unborn children. Eco-imbalance is not compatible with existence, we either retrace our steps or risk an entire nation go into extinction. It is time for every Nigerian to contribute to building and sustaining an eco-friendly lifestyle that will perpetuate our survival and create for our unborn children an environment they will love to call home. This therefore presents a huge business opportunity for savvy entrepreneurs to come up with eco-friendly solutions to the environmental problems of Nigeria.

ECONOMIC SUSTAINABILITY

As stated earlier, Sustainable Development is the development that meets the needs of the present without compromising the ability of the future generations to meet their needs. In economic terms, sustainability concerns the specification of a set of actions to be taken by present persons that will not diminish the prospects of future persons to enjoy levels of consumption, wealth, utility, or welfare comparable to those enjoyed by present persons. The future generation of Nigerians stands at a risk of bankruptcy, if the present rate of lavish payment to the Nigerian legislature continues. Nigeria's legislatures are one of the highest paid in the world, while Nigerian minimum wage is one of the lowest in the world. How sustainable is an economy that spends almost all its budget on recurrent expenditure, with little left to finance infrastructure development for the future generation? Resources have limits, but within every resource is a seed that will help perpetuate present level consumption to the next generation. A society that has no investment plan to support the future is only setting the stage for economic woes. How can a country that is in dire need of infrastructural development pay so much for its legislature?

Between 2004 and 2010, Nigeria's economy grew at an average of 7.2% while at the same time absolute poverty went up by 6.4%. If growth is not distributed more evenly among the population, then how sustainable is that economic growth? The development of a nation is measured in terms of how it takes care of its down trodden, less privileged and vulnerable groups. How can a country that has more than 60% of its population living on less than $2 per day, be paying his legislatures in the million USD range per annum? How sustainable is an economy that spends almost all its resources on the few elites? This is a mindset issue. Even in business sector, until recently we focus only on the few elites that have the means to pay for the so called *'high class goods and services'*, we build estates and properties only the top income earners can afford. We have created a society only elites can thrive, ignoring the majority at the bottom of the pyramid, who also yearns for the same quality of life.

We were ignorant of the fact that right at the bottom of the pyramid is fortune for the savvy entrepreneurs. Gradually, the tides are changing, investors globally now realize the huge opportunity for returns in churning out affordable products and services to meet the vacuum of needs at the bottom of the pyramid. Unfortunately Nigerians are still oblivious of the fact that a business can deliver world class quality to the masses and still stay profitable. That is the growth plan of many fortune 500 companies operating in Nigeria, flooding the market with popularly positioned product (PPP) and services, with a goal of having double digit growth difficult to find elsewhere. An economy can only be sustainable if it does not exclude lower social strata of the society from participating, because they are the engine of real growth.

NIGERIA A LAND OF OPPORTUNITIES!

Nigeria is a land of opportunities! Nigeria is another name for opportunities! We step on them in the street corners, and on every highway, but we fail to see them as opportunities. We complain about the Nigerian problems but we fail to realize that they are opportunities in disguise! We know the ABC of the problems; we even debate them among our friends and colleagues. Some people got so frustrated of the problems that they saddle their horse in search of diamonds in the far country ending up in a life of deeper misery, too ashamed and poor to come back home! What a pity!

While some people are lamenting about the problems, some others are capitalizing on them to become multinational giants right on the soil of Nigeria! While Africans are lamenting about their problems, the global investment community is salivating at the world's juiciest investment opportunity this continent presents. Are you also going to saddle your horse to go for diamond search in foreign lands or will you settle down to exploit the vast untapped opportunities staring you in the face in Nigeria? The choice is yours to make!

By now, most investors and businesses know about the tremendous potential of Africa— the world's second-fastest-growing region, topped only by emerging Asia. Africa's growth is fuelled not by resources but rather by a rising consumer market. The continent's consumer-facing industries are expected to grow by $400 billion, representing its single-largest business opportunity, by 2020. One of the factors shaping this new consuming class is Africa's population, the fastest growing and youngest in the world, concentrated in urban areas. This new class of consumer has a smaller family, is better educated and higher earning, and is digitally savvy.

You must not be a latecomer to discovering the huge business and investment opportunities in Nigeria. The whole world is beginning to see these opportunities. Virtually in every sector, you see multinational firms investing in such a huge scale we have never seen before. Indeed, you can't get away from the fundamentals of this country – 170 million people with tremendous natural wealth and an unbelievable entrepreneur spirit. There's huge opportunity around the continent of Africa, but I have to say that the opportunity is of a different order of magnitude in Nigeria. If Nigeria must be one of the world's top 20 economies within the next 20 years, I personally believe thatat every Nigerian must begin to tap into these opportunities by creating new services and products to solve the numerous problems in every sector.

Nigeria has hither to been starved of value. But entrepreneurs of the future will become focused on delivering value. The Nigerian products and services that have been known for inferiority will soon be known for the best of quality. This is the future; let's go there together! Nigerian consumers must not turn again to the western world for quality products and services. But, it all depends on you to give them the quality and excellence they deserve. There is indeed a unique opportunity for those who will be committed to delivering value to Nigerians. Nigeria is indeed a land of opportunities!

REFRENCES

1. Conwell R.H. Acres of Diamond
2. 2 Corinthians 4:7 King James Version of the Holy Bible.
3. Genesis 2:8, 15-16 King James Version of the Holy Bible.
4. Acts 10:34-35 King James Version of the Holy Bible.
5. Romans 10:12 King James Version of the Holy Bible.
6. Ecclesiastes 5:9 King James Version of the Holy Bible.
7. 'Nigeria-Country Brief'. Web. Worldbank.org. 2011-09-23. Retrieved 2012-03-21
8. 'Nigeria'. DFID. Retrieved 2012-03-21.
9. 'GDP (Current US$)'. World Bank. Retrieved July 2, 2013
10. Genesis 13:14-15 King James Version of the Holy Bible.
11. Proverb 29:18 King James Version of the Holy Bible.
12. Proverb 11:3 King James Version of the Holy Bible.
13. Proverb 8:22-24 King James Version of the Holy Bible.
14. The Times Magazine, January 13, 1997 edition, page 34.
15. Mlkec<./inventory/abbrev.htm>. Back to Top@ The Estate of Martin Luther King, Jr.<./copyright.htm.
16. King James Version of the Holy Bible.
17. Matthew 19:30 King James Version of the Holy Bible.
18. Genesis 9:7-12 King James Version of the Holy Bible.
19. Genesis 11:5 King James Version of the Holy Bible.
20. Wilmington's guide to the Bible, by Dr D.H.L. Wilmington. Tyndale House Publishers Inc Wheaton, Illinois.
21. Leonard Karshima Shilgba, @ 1999-2004 Nigeriaworld.com.
22. Genesis 11:3-6 King James Version of the Holy Bible.
23. Genesis 30:37-41   King James Version of the Holy Bible.
24. Proverb 23:7 King James Version of the Holy Bible.
25. The Principles and Power of Vision @ 2003 By Dr Myles Munroe
26. Jeremiah 1:11-12 King James Version of the Holy Bible.
27. Genesis 37:5-9 King James Version of the Holy Bible.
28. Genesis 37:19-20 King James Version of the Holy Bible.
29. Genesis 42:6-9 King James Version of the Holy Bible.
30. Habakkuk 2:1-2 King James Version of the Holy Bible.
31. Numbers 13:30 King James Version of the Holy Bible.
32. Nehemiah 1:3-4; 2:1-6 King James Version of the Holy Bible.
33. 1 Samuel 17:23-26 King James Version of the Holy Bible.
34. Matthew 6:32-33 King James Version of the Holy Bible.

35. Business Masterminds : Bill Gates, Genius of the Software
    Revolution and Master of The Information Age @ 2000
    Robert Heller
36. http://www.forbes.com/profile/bill-gates/
37. Proverb 11:24-25 King James Version of the Holy Bible.
38. Genesis 12: 2 King James Version of the Holy Bible.
39. Luke 22:24-27 King James Version of the Holy Bible.
40. Amos 6:1 King James Version of the Holy Bible.
41. John 2:13-17 King James Version of the Holy Bible.
42. Genesis 1:28 King James Version of the Holy Bible.
43. Romans 8:19-21 King James Version of the Holy Bible.
44. Proverbs 13:23 King James Version of the Holy Bible.
45. '2012 Form 10-K, Wal-Mart Stores, Inc.'. Google
46. Luke 6:38 King James Version of the Holy Bible.
47. Isaiah 5:1-6 King James Version of the Holy Bible.
48. Proverb 18:16 King James Version of the Holy Bible.
49. Proverb 22:29 King James Version of the Holy Bible.
50. Genesis 1:2 King James Version of the Holy Bible.
51. Proverb 20:27 King James Version of the Holy Bible.
52. Job 32:8 King James Version of the Holy Bible.
53. Daniel 5:11-12 King James Version of the Holy Bible.
54. Psalm 24:1 King James Version of the Holy Bible.
55. Matthew 22:37-40 King James Version of the Holy Bible.
56. 1 John 4:20 King James Version of the Holy Bible.
57. http://www.cia.gov/cia/publications/factbook/geos/my.html
58. Luke 19:12-26 King James Version of the Holy Bible.
59. Haggai 2:8 King James Version of the Holy Bible.
60. Proverb 10:4 King James Version of the Holy Bible.
61. Matthew 13:31-32 King James Version of the Holy Bible.
62. Ecclesiastes 3:1-2 King James Version of the Holy Bible.
63. Psalm 112:1-5 King James Version of the Holy Bible
64. Proverb 21:17 King James Version of the Holy Bible.
65. John 6:5-13 King James Version of the Holy Bible.
66. Psalm 31:15 King James Version of the Holy Bible.
67. Romans 8:28-29 King James Version of the Holy Bible.
68. Ecclesiastes 3:11 King James Version of the Holy Bible.
69. Ephesians 5:15-16 King James Version of the Holy Bible.
70. Psalm 23:6 King James Version of the Holy Bible.
71. The Times Magazine, January 13, 1997 edition, page 32
72. Proverb 14:34 King James Version of the Holy Bible.
73.

74. Romans 12:1 King James Version of the Holy Bible.
75. Proverb 14:34 King James Version of the Holy Bible.
76. Genesis 41:39-41 King James Version of the Holy Bible.
77. Genesis 39:7-9 King James Version of the Holy Bible.
78. Job 22:23-25 King James Version of the Holy Bible.
79. Proverb 1:23 King James Version of the Holy Bible.
80. Isaiah 45:2-3 King James Version of the Holy Bible.
81. Proverb 13:22 King James Version of the Holy Bible.
82. Matthew 25:15-16 King James Version of the Holy Bible.
83. 1 Kings 4:29:34 King James Version of the Holy Bible.
84. 1 Kings 10:23-25 King James Version of the Holy Bible.
85. Proverbs 24:3-4 the living Bible Translation.
86. Song of Solomon 1:6 King James Version of the Holy Bible.

ABOUT THE AUTHOR

Tobi Kehinde Ilesanmi holds a Bachelor of Medicine and Bachelor of Surgery (MBBS) degree from the University of Ilorin. Tobi works for the world's leading Nutrition, Health and Wellness company. In his spare time, he is an Independent Consultant for leading multinationals in the financial services, FMCG and other key sectors of the Nigerian and African economy. His passion is to make significant contribution to the transformation of African economies from third world to first world. He runs SIYON Corporate Business Limited with his wife and a blog- 'Brand Nigeria' at 'www.brandnigeria-oluwatobiloba.blogspot'. You can follow him on Twitter @brandnigeria and on Facebook at 'Nigeria: A Land of Opportunities'.